Literacy Strategies for Gifted and Accelerated Readers

Literacy Strategies for Gifted and Accelerated Readers

Vicki Caruana

ROWMAN & LITTLEFIELD
Lanham • Boulder • New York • London

Published by Rowman & Littlefield
An imprint of The Rowman & Littlefield Publishing Group, Inc.
4501 Forbes Boulevard, Suite 200, Lanham, Maryland 20706
www.rowman.com

6 Tinworth Street, London SE11 5AL

British Library Cataloguing in Publication Information Available

Library of Congress Cataloging-in-Publication Data

Names: Caruana, Vicki, author.
Title: Literacy strategies for gifted and accelerated readers / Vicki Caruana.
Description: Lanham : Rowman & Littlefield, [2020] | Includes bibliographical references. | Summary: "This book provides teachers who have one or more gifted/accelerated or those who are 'keenly interested' students in their class ways in which they can differentiate reading instruction that is equitable"—Provided by publisher.
Identifiers: LCCN 2019039257 (print) | LCCN 2019039258 (ebook) | ISBN 9781475847093 (cloth) | ISBN 9781475847109 (paperback) | ISBN 9781475847116 (epub)
Subjects: LCSH: Reading (Elementary)—United States. | Gifted children—Education—United States. | Gifted children—Books and reading—United States.
Classification: LCC LC3993.5 .C37 2020 (print) | LCC LC3993.5 (ebook) | DDC 372.4—dc23
LC record available at https://lccn.loc.gov/2019039257
LC ebook record available at https://lccn.loc.gov/2019039258

For my first class of gifted sixth graders in our literature class at Safety Harbor Middle School—you may be grown and gone from my sight, but not forgotten.

Contents

Foreword

It is not a secret! Gifted and advanced learners are the most neglected students in our classrooms. The myth that these students "will get it on their own" still runs rampant. It is true that many will continue to progress by their own self-directed instruction, but what have they—and society—lost in not receiving guidance and instruction to become critical and creative learners at a very advanced level? This lack of challenge is especially true in the area of reading and literacy. Many of these students receive little or no instruction in reading, let alone exposure to advanced reading instruction!

For years, I have pushed the idea that reading programs for gifted and advanced readers should be based upon the concept that these students should *read to learn not learn to read*. In Dr. Caruana's *Literacy Strategies for Gifted and Accelerated Readers*, we find this sentiment beautifully stated, supported, and developed. In addition, she provides clear and concise guidelines for teachers to build appropriately differentiated and challenging reading programs for gifted and advanced readers. The format of the book lends itself well to the university classroom or as a self-directed course to help teachers meet the needs of these unique students. Another strength of *Literacy Strategies* is that it gathers, summarizes, and synthesizes current research related to the gifted and reading by citing the works, among others, of Halsted, Reis, and Wood.

Caruana's statement: *Teachers cannot and should not attempt to employ typical curriculum and instruction with atypical learners* provides an insight that is most important and is often overlooked. Uniqueness requires a unique response. *Literacy Strategies* answers the reality of the scarcity of practical, research-based resources that provide the challenge that is imperative for gifted and advanced readers and provides guidelines and strategies for classroom teachers. This is an important contribution to the field.

These eight chapters provide a wealth of information, guidelines, and strategies. I think most teachers are aware that they need to provide different and appropriate reading instruction for their gifted and advanced readers but they often ask: "How do I go about doing this?" *Literacy Strategies for Gifted and Accelerated Readers* clearly answers this question. While it is difficult and perhaps impossible to point out the most important concepts, I found chapter 3 to be especially important: We must debunk the myths about gifted learners and gifted readers. This, as Caruana points out, is key in appropriately serving gifted readers. She not only debunks the myths, but she gives valuable, reliable, and easy to follow guidelines on what to do. In addition, the importance of chapters 5, 6, and 7 on creative reading, critical reading, and inquiry reading cannot be over empathized. These three chapters alone are reason enough that *Literacy Strategies for Gifted and Accelerated Readers* should be in the hands of teachers.

I am confident that the reader will be informed, encouraged, and enlightened and will enjoy this reading adventure as much as I did! Happy Reading!

Dr. Bob Seney

Professor Emeritus/Gifted Studies

Mississippi University for Women

Chapter One

How to Use This Book

Literacy instruction, including reading instruction across the content areas, is integral to student success. Gifted readers who have already mastered the foundational skills in reading require specially designed instruction in order to make progress and meet their potential. Teachers cannot and should not attempt to employ a typical curriculum and instruction with atypical learners. Gifted readers by definition have a reading ability above the norm of their peers. Differentiation of instruction, when appropriately designed, effectively meets the needs of all children. Whether teachers are prepared to differentiate is another question. This book demystifies the necessary differentiation for gifted readers.

Each chapter opens with a scenario that illustrates the need for a different set of strategies for gifted readers. Sometimes the scenario paints a picture, sometimes it poses a problem, and sometimes it poses a problem with a possible solution. As you consider each scenario, try to recognize a context, a student, or even yourself in the story. It sets the stage for the story and lesson in the rest of the chapter.

The following elements are included in each chapter to take the reader and teacher through a lesson-like experience: An overview leads into an exposition of the different literacy strategies found to work well with gifted readers. Then, each chapter offers the chance to learn, apply, and reflect on the strategies. Many of the chapters also include valuable insights on the topic from renowned experts in gifted education, who add their own wisdom to the discussion on literacy differentiation for gifted readers.

THE STRATEGIES

Each chapter addresses ways in which teachers can differentiate literacy instruction to meet the needs of gifted readers. These strategies are identified from decades of research on differentiation for gifted students in traditional or inclusive classrooms. It is not an exhaustive list of appropriate strategies, but it offers teachers a starting point in their quest to meet the needs of all learners.

THE ASSIGNMENTS

Teachers have the opportunity to apply what they learn in each chapter with assignments. When this book is included as a text in a college course on curriculum and instruction for gifted students, these assignments can supplement other course assignments.

THE REFLECTIONS

Each chapter concludes by giving teachers an opportunity to reflect on what they've learned. The reflection may be a question to help teachers dig deeper into their own instructional decision making or one that spurs them forward to take a risk in their own teaching.

FROM THE EXPERTS

Where appropriate and where most effective, experts in gifted education with an emphasis on reading were interviewed or asked to provide relevant content to extend the learning for teachers. These are strong voices in literacy and gifted education who are in effect guest lecturers in this book.

The chapters in this book represent a scope of literacy strategies for gifted readers but do not represent a sequence. They do not have to be read or considered in order. Each is able to stand alone in its assertions. I anticipate that readers will read to learn (and not learn to read), just like every gifted reader. What area is most relevant to you at the moment? Learn about it and know that the rest is available for your consumption when needed.

Chapter Two

Overview of Literacy Instruction

"The more that you read, the more things you will know. The more that you learn, the more places you'll go."—Dr. Seuss

SCENARIO

Ms. French has loved being a first-grade teacher for the past 10 years. It offers her ample opportunities to instill foundational reading and writing skills in these newly minted first graders. Phonological awareness, basic word recognition, basic print concepts, and basic language skills make up most of her scope and sequence for the year.

Beyond the basics, Ms. French wants her students to enjoy school; she wants them to have fun and feel confident in their learning. She knows that, in kindergarten, her students didn't enter on the first day of school at the same level of competence. Some children have developmental delays. Others had not been read to by their parents. Still others had never before been expected to attend to a grown-up for more than a couple minutes and spent kindergarten learning the necessary "school" behaviors. There is a lot of variety to her learners and therefore a lot to plan for. And then in walks Christopher.

Christopher is a first grader reading on a fifth-grade level. He reads for both pleasure and information on his own. The library is his second home. No other student in Ms. French's classroom comes anywhere close to his reading level. The basics would be lost on him, but there are other aspects of literacy that Christopher needs to learn.

He is developmentally on par with writing, for example. His comprehension skills are higher than his peers' but with room to grow. His speaking and listening skills are also higher than his peers', but Ms. French could work

with that, as well. If this student is well beyond the basics of literacy instruction, then determining how and where to begin is Ms. French's challenge.
Starting at the beginning is out of the question. For this one student, does she
have to follow a completely separate path?

The basics of literacy instruction are the foundation on which advanced or
accelerated literacy instruction are designed and built. Differentiation of curriculum, instruction, and assessment are only effective when you first understand the generalized curriculum content knowledge. Professional educators
agree that, as the starting point, all students need to learn content and skills,
whether they appear in the form of national or state standards or foundational
skills from the National Reading Panel. These minimum standards and skills
are necessary to create a literate student population. Gifted and accelerated
readers, however, often have already met these minimum standards and
skills. They are often already literate.

In this chapter, I explore the five components of literacy instruction and
unpack them in a way that is applicable to gifted and accelerated readers. I
also outline some of the best practices in literacy instruction and include an
overview of the features of an effective literacy program for gifted and accelerated readers.

REVISITING THE FIVE ESSENTIAL COMPONENTS OF LITERACY INSTRUCTION

The National Reading Panel (NICHD, 2000) outlines five components that
have been used almost exclusively as the foundation of literacy instruction
since the early 2000s. These components form the mechanics of literacy.
Often, gifted readers have already learned the basics (mechanics) of reading
and writing and are therefore ready for higher-order literacies (Knight, 2001).
The following is an overview of the five components of basic literacy.

1. Phonemic Awareness

Phonemic awareness is important when learning to read and has been used as
a predictor of how well students read (NICHD, 2000). The emphasis is on the
ability to recognize and manipulate phonemes in words. For example, the
word *bat* has three sounds (or phonemes): /b/ /a/ /t/.

Phonemic awareness is not, however, an isolated skill. It is developed in
conjunction with more difficult skills, such as word attack. Students use the
sounds at the beginnings, middles, and ends of words to blend into real and
nonsense words. They are used in rhyming and word-recognition skills
where a sound is substituted or omitted. Systematic instruction is most commonly used to teach phonemic awareness.

The Gifted Reader. Differentiating for gifted readers in the primary grades presents unique challenges. As teachers focus on their students' ability to master letter names and letter sounds, they can attend to the needs of gifted readers by changing the context for them. For example, if students are learning about the letter name and sound of /b/, give gifted readers the challenge of a letter name and sound scavenger hunt. They can identify people, places, things, or ideas in the classroom or school that begin or end with /b/.

2. Phonics

Phonics is a set of rules for how letters and sounds interact in spelling and spoken language. These rules help students decode unfamiliar words that are not sight words and are consistent enough to help struggling readers (Foorman, Francis, Fletcher, Schatschneider, & Mehta, 1998). Although not all teachers use phonics instruction, the logical rules inherent in phonics offer the emerging reader a structure that supports decoding. Once students know letter names and sounds, they can put them together in a meaningful way. For example, phonics instruction helps readers translate the distinct letter sounds /b/ /a/ /t/ into the word *bat*.

The Gifted Reader. Gifted readers often already understand the nuances of language and use multiple strategies to decode unfamiliar words without additional instruction. For those who learned letter names and sounds early, they can take the next step (phonics) to combine those letter sounds meaningfully on their own. While other students are still struggling to increase their word recognition using different word-attack strategies, gifted readers are ready to move onto reading on their own.

The connection of phonics to fluency (see the next section) is assessed by a collection of different measures. Teachers discover that their advanced or gifted readers often are at the top achievement of those measures. This is an indicator that the gifted reader needs more, not less, advanced instruction in reading.

3. Fluency

The basic definition of *fluency* is accuracy plus rate plus expression of word recognition. It is often measured by reading inventories or curriculum-based measures (e.g., DIBELS, Teachers College Running Records, iReady, DOLCH or FRY sight word lists). Fluent readers engage in automaticity, where they spend less energy decoding and more energy comprehending. Fluency is a prerequisite for more advanced reading skills. The process used to gain fluency is usually repeated readings and the use of basal or leveled readers.

The Gifted Reader. Gifted readers are, more often than not, fluent readers. They have already met the foundational reading skills included in national or state content standards. The focus for gifted readers at this stage is to apply the basic skills they've already learned up to this point. They do not need guided repeated readings, so basal or leveled readers are not appropriate for their advanced needs. The emphasis should not be on building fluency but instead on analysis, synthesis, and evaluation as they apply their fluency to different genres (Knight, 2001).

4. Vocabulary

Vocabulary is important for comprehension and is one of the most crucial components for making meaning of both oral and written communication. Children connect their understanding of words from their own oral communication bank to unfamiliar vocabulary they encounter. A well-stocked oral vocabulary makes learning new vocabulary less challenging. Vocabulary should be taught on a regular, long-term basis. Teaching vocabulary during prereading is especially important (Brett, Rothlein, & Hurley, 1996). Vocabulary acquisition is the linchpin for comprehension and overall reading achievement.

The Gifted Reader. One of the defining characteristics of gifted readers is a robust vocabulary that allows them to comprehend advanced texts. Early acquisition of vocabulary sets them apart from other readers. Traditional approaches to teaching vocabulary focus on a surface examination of word meaning. Gifted readers benefit from a deeper exploration of word meaning and usage.

Consider focusing on multiple-meaning words and homophones. Study the etymology of words and examine their Greek or Latin roots. Compare the use of idioms and proper English. Compare English vocabulary to the vocabulary in other languages. Think about word relationships by teaching analogies.

5. Comprehension

Comprehension is the final stage of reading instruction. It is a synthesis of all the prior components to basic literacy. This is where students make meaning by connecting what they read to what they already know. When reading proficiency is assessed, it is assessed at the comprehension level. Consider the achievement-level description of "proficient" from the National Assessment of Educational Progress:

> Fourth-grade students performing at the *Proficient* level should be able to integrate and interpret texts and apply their understanding of the text to draw conclusions and make evaluations.

When reading literary texts such as fiction, poetry, and literary nonfiction, fourth-grade students performing at the *Proficient* level should be able to identify implicit main ideas and recognize relevant information that supports them. Students should be able to judge elements of author's craft and provide some support for their judgment. They should be able to analyze character roles, actions, feelings, and motives.

When reading informational texts such as articles and excerpts from books, fourth-grade students performing at the *Proficient* level should be able to locate relevant information, integrate information across texts, and evaluate the way an author presents information. Student performance at this level should demonstrate an understanding of the purpose for text features and an ability to integrate information from headings, text boxes, graphics and their captions. They should be able to explain a simple cause-and-effect relationship and draw conclusions. (NAEP, 2017)

The most recent NAEP report card on reading suggests that two out of three students do not perform at the proficient level. Only one third perform at the proficient or higher level (i.e., advanced). As a result, the instructional emphasis for literacy has been and continues to be on the lowest 25% of readers still operating at the basic level or below.

The Gifted Reader. Gifted and advanced readers gain little, if anything, from the core reading curriculum in today's schools. Many of these readers developed their reading skills outside of school and show up already reading (Jackson, 1993). At this point, the emphasis shouldn't be on making readers but on helping gifted readers to advance their reading abilities, to synthesize what they already know, and to make deep connections.

A CLASSROOM OBSERVATION

Many teachers, although highly qualified and prepared to teach reading to beginning and struggling readers, are not prepared to meet the reading needs of their gifted and accelerated readers. Consider this scenario (adapted from Wood, 2008):

> It's 9:20 a.m. on a Tuesday in Ms. Markel's second-grade class. During an unannounced "walk-through" to observe the reading block, Mr. Watson, the school principal, observes children involved in a variety of reading activities around the room. Ms. Markel sits at a table with a guided reading group focused on word attack and decoding unfamiliar words.
>
> The principal sees Justin, Jaime, and Stephanie sitting at computers using the iReady reading intervention program. Under a jungle-themed tent in the reading corner, Fabio is reading slowly but surely to Mandy, who gives him assistance when he struggles with a word. Joe, Dustin, and Sara are at their desks independently writing in their journals, while Karen and Mike are at the "Build-a-Word" center using multisensory items to create words. In the back

corner on comfy beanbag chairs, Charlie, Megan, and Maria sit reading silently.

During the principal's visit, he notices that the current groupings switch to another activity every 20 minutes—all except for Charlie, Megan, and Maria, who continue to read silently in their comfy beanbag chairs. Mr. Watson is curious about why these three students do not experience the different activities and groupings during their reading block.

Later, during Ms. Markel's postobservation conference, Mr. Watson says, "I noticed that Charlie, Megan, and Maria continued to read silently while the rest of the students had the opportunity to rotate to other activities and groupings. Why is that?" Without hesitancy, Ms. Markel responds, "Oh, they are my top readers. They already know how to read, so I've told them to just read their books."

Sadly, this scenario is all too familiar in classrooms across the country. Gifted and accelerated readers are often left out of reading instruction. They deserve a reading program that offers challenges and is differentiated based on their intellectual and emotional needs (Wood, 2008).

BEYOND THE FIVE COMPONENTS

The emphasis on the five components of literacy instruction consumes much of a classroom teacher's time and energy. Their planning focuses solely on teaching either to the middle or lower 25% of readers in order to meet the needs of and show growth for the majority of their students. Majority is not *all*. Majority is *most*. Approximately 9% of readers achieve at the advanced level (NAEP, 2017), which translate to approximately 3 students out of a class of 30. The needs of 3 students, especially if they are not a behavior problem, are often easy to overlook.

Conversely it may be just as easy to plan for and address the needs of three advanced or gifted readers in your classroom. How might teachers address the needs of advanced or gifted readers and still address the five components of literacy instruction? Each of the five components of literacy can be addressed for advanced or gifted readers through acceleration or curriculum compacting, enrichment, technology, grouping, advanced questioning, and student choice. Consider Table 2.1 for ideas.

BEST CLASSROOM PRACTICES IN
LITERACY INSTRUCTION FOR GIFTED READERS

Reading to learn is the focus of literacy instruction for gifted and advanced readers who already have learned to read. There are several ways to facilitate reading to learn for gifted readers. Examine and plan using the standards to determine which offer depth and complexity. Use flexible groupings to target

Table 2.1. Literacy Components and Gifted Readers

Literacy Component	How to Address the Needs of Gifted Readers
Phonemic Awareness	Use curriculum compacting and acceleration because these students already have robust phonemic awareness.
Phonics	If phonics is already well established, use high-interest trade books instead of basal readers.
Fluency	Fluency is often already established for gifted readers; however, an emphasis on reading with expression using poetry or readers' theater is recommended.
Vocabulary	The advanced or gifted reader often already has an extensive vocabulary, evident through both oral and written communication. An emphasis on morphology (word origins) and syntax that extends their use of vocabulary is an effective approach.
Comprehension	Because reading assessment is often conducted at the comprehension level, readers who have been identified as advanced have basic comprehension down. At this point teachers can help them to synthesize what they already know and to make deep connections. They are reading to learn instead of learning to read, so use varied texts and texts chosen by the readers to answer questions, solve problems, or create something new.

instruction to shared needed skills. Provide access to rich, high-interest, and more complex reading material. Facilitate independent investigations for students to apply their research skills. These classroom practices may be employed organically by teachers who are student centered; however, when confronted with one or more gifted readers in your classroom, you must be intentional in targeting and then choosing effective practices to meet the needs of your students.

These classroom practices are explored in more depth in the chapters that follow. Just as the classroom practices of teachers should be differentiated for gifted readers, so must the reading program itself.

FEATURES OF A LITERACY PROGRAM FOR GIFTED READERS

A reading or literacy program adopted by a particular school or district does not always capture the unique needs of all of the students with whom it will be used. Although we can critically analyze a reading program to see how well it addresses the five pillars of literacy, how effective it is for primary readers and English-language learners, and whether there is sufficient supplementary instruction for those requiring reading intervention, we don't der the needs of gifted or advanced readers in our adoption pro-

features might be considered in a literacy program for gifted read-
ɔu cannot find the following in an already-published program, then it
woulɑ ɓe prudent to include these program goals alongside the program
adopted by your school or district. The following eight program goals differentiate the reading experience for gifted readers from those who struggle to
read:

1. Expose students to challenging reading material.
2. Deepen reading comprehension skills.
3. Expand students' metacognitive processes during reading.
4. Develop critical reading, including interpretation and analysis of text.
5. Foster an appreciation of diverse, multicultural literature across multiple genres.
6. Provide opportunities for group discussion of selected texts.
7. Encourage creative reading behaviors, including writing and dramatic
   interpretation.
8. Promote motivation and enjoyment of reading through choice and
   self-selection of texts (Wood, 2008, p. 20).

In the following chapters, I present what these program goals look like when
employed in a classroom with gifted or keenly interested learners.

* * *

From the Experts
*Sally Reis, author, vice provost for academic affairs, a board of trustees
distinguished professor, and a teaching fellow in educational psychology at
the University of Connecticut*

In the last decade, my colleagues and I have contributed to the scholarly
research on talented readers and have synthesized several broad themes about
the definitions of talented readers, finding that talented readers are most often
characterized by reading early and at advanced levels, using advanced processing in reading, reading with enthusiasm and enjoyment, and demonstrat-
ing advanced language skills (oral, reading, and written).

In more recent work, we have also found that some talented readers
display higher levels of self-regulation than do other students, suggesting that
they are able to independently focus on challenging reading for longer peri-
ods of time, display higher levels of control of classroom movement, and
show more efficient book-selection behaviors.

We have seen a decrease in practices challenging talented and gifted readers. Our research strongly finds that few teachers differentiate for talented readers and instead focus on those who read below grade level. Differentiation in reading is challenging and often simply too difficult for many teachers to implement, and reading levels are increasingly widening in regular and gifted classrooms at the elementary and middle school levels.

My colleagues and I used in-depth qualitative comparative case studies to study 12 third- through seventh-grade reading classrooms in urban and suburban schools. Our observations of daily practices in reading classrooms were used to determine frequency and type of various differentiation practices, such as curriculum compacting, interest or instructional-level grouping arrangements, acceleration opportunities, and the nature of independent reading or work completed by talented readers. These observations indicated that talented readers received some minimal levels of differentiated reading instruction in only 3 of the 12 classrooms.

In the other nine classrooms, no challenging reading material or advanced instruction was provided for talented readers during regular classroom reading instruction. Appropriately challenging books were seldom made available for talented students, and they were rarely provided with more challenging work. Different patterns did emerge across urban and suburban school districts; the three classroom teachers who provided some level of differentiation taught in suburban schools.

At the elementary level, it appears that teachers are still solely focused on the five components of literacy instruction (phonemic awareness, phonics, fluency, vocabulary, comprehension). But their gifted readers have already mastered those skills. The need to compact curriculum for talented readers is crucial, given our recent research on the range of reading fluency and comprehension scores of 1,149 students in five diverse elementary schools, including a gifted and talented magnet school.

A broad range was found in reading comprehension across all schools, including 9.2 grade levels in Grade 3, 11.3 in Grade 4, and 11.6 in Grade 5. A similar wide range of oral reading fluency scores was found across all elementary schools, as students scored from below the 10th percentile to above the 90th percentile. These results demonstrate the wide range of reading achievement in diverse populations of students, including gifted students in a self-contained school for gifted students, who had the broadest range of comprehension. The research also strongly suggests the crucial need for teachers to differentiate both reading content and instruction to enable all students to make continuous progress in reading.

We found that teachers who used curriculum compacting could eliminate 40% to 50% of the regular reading curriculum for advanced readers with no change to standardized achievement test scores. Teachers in a follow-up to this study extended the use of curriculum compacting to students who were not identified as gifted and to some students who had learning disabilities, with similar favorable results.

Teachers should challenge gifted and talented readers by using instructional grouping and enabling students to read more advanced content in their areas of interest. These students should be challenged by reading-workshop questions that enable them to consider more depth and complexity of responses. In essence, we suggest that they use the methods that we describe in the Schoolwide Enrichment Model-Reading (SEM-R).

The goals of the SEM-R are to increase reading achievement and self-regulation strategies through increased interest and motivation. In phase 1, teachers stimulate interest in reading by engaging students through book talks and interesting read-alouds of a variety of genres, followed by scaffolding of higher-level questions.

During phase 2, also called supported independent reading, students read silently from self-selected materials at appropriate levels of challenge, and teachers conduct individualized, differentiated reading conferences with students. During this time, teachers assess students' comprehension using higher-order questions and ensure that students are reading books that are adequately challenging.

The third phase enables students to choose a pleasurable reading activity or project based on their interests from a menu of choices, such as independent study, creativity training activities, books on tape or CD, reading alone or with a friend, using technology, or doing interesting self-selected short-term projects.

Schools or districts can include the needs of their top readers in their curriculum and instruction priorities in a variety of ways. They can do this by having policies adopted by the board of education that include the need to challenge and differentiate instruction for all students and to group students by achievement levels for reading.

For teachers who are realizing for the first time that they must address the needs of their gifted readers, I recommend using the SEM-R. The SEM-R has been implemented in hundreds of regular and gifted classrooms. Research using experimental designs has compared the performance of students who use the SEM-R enrichment approach to reading instruction with a control group of students who participated in basal reading programs. Students who participated in this differentiated reading approach had significantly higher or similar scores in reading fluency, comprehension, and attitudes toward reading when compared to students in the control group. This demonstrates that talented readers, as well as average and below-average readers, benefit from the SEM-R intervention.

When differentiated, enriched reading instruction is implemented, students' reading fluency and comprehension has been found to be as high as or higher than a control group that used a traditional whole-group instructional basal reading approach. Our research suggests that talented readers benefit from challenging materials in reading based on their interests and the opportunity to tackle appropriate substitute books that offer complexity and challenge their comprehension and fluency.

It also suggests that talented readers can be given opportunities to complete different creative projects and participate in alternative writing assignments. They can be encouraged to bring prior knowledge and insight into their interpretations of challenging text. They can use technology to access websites of authors, read challenging books online, and interact with talented readers from other schools using literature-circle discussion strategies. Technology has been found to be an outstanding tool for accessing advanced content; creating concept maps and other technological products; and writing and revising stories, chapters, and even books.

The SEM-R instructional strategies for differentiating instruction and curriculum for talented readers can be used in combination to provide an enriching, advanced reading program. For example, curriculum compacting uses assessment that may lead to advanced content and products for students. This strategy, however, requires teachers to find appropriately challenging resources and materials and may also require classroom changes, such as the creation of a space for students to work together and for providing advanced content materials.

All students should have opportunities to participate in appropriately challenging learning experiences, and differentiated instruction can be used to ensure that all learners experience continuous progress in reading. Teaching reading with one set of materials that the majority of students in a heterogeneous classroom can read will undoubtedly create boredom for talented readers and should be discouraged as a practice. If teachers continue to use basal textbooks or even the same three or four class sets of grade-level novels to teach all students, then diminished achievement in reading will occur for talented readers, particularly in urban or low socioeconomic areas, where remedial and direct instruction are too often used for all students.

* * *

Let's revisit Ms. Markel's second-grade class to see what an improved reading program would look like for Charlie, Megan, and Maria:

> Ms. Markel adjusts her reading centers to incorporate options for inquiry and independent research, creative reading tasks, and more challenging literature. The centers offer several levels of challenge and are available to all her students, not just Charlie, Megan, and Maria.
>
> Ms. Markel has begun including her top readers in a guided-reading group to encourage more complex thinking about the text and to teach analysis skills for story structure and author intent. Charlie, Megan, and Maria no longer

spend the entire reading block alone in the corner reading silently. They participate in flexible groups, work with Junior Great Books for above-grade-level readers, and are given choices in what they want to read and how they want to respond to what they read.

Charlie, who is an amateur astronomer, scours the internet for the latest reports from the Mars rover that he can add to his presentation for the science fair, while Megan and Maria work on a collaborative book of short stories they hope to have published and available in the school's library. Here, we see that Charlie is engaged in inquiry reading on a topic that fascinates him. The use of Junior Great Books and the Socratic questioning method help build more critical reading during guided reading.

ASSIGNMENT

Review the literacy components in Table 2.1 and consider how to differentiate them for gifted readers. Then consider the eight literacy program goals for gifted readers. Inspect your own classroom library, and redesign it using both the literacy components and program goals for gifted readers. Describe the changes you could make and the rationale for your changes in order to meet the needs of gifted readers in your classroom.

CONCLUSION

It's a mistake to believe that, if gifted and advanced readers are already fluent and know how to read, then they no longer need reading instruction. Part of the challenge is realizing that the decision of whether to plan for needs of specific students depends on what teachers believe to be true about those learners. Do they in fact need additional or specially designed instruction? Will they thrive regardless of our intervention? Will they read to learn on their own because they have already learned to read? Chapter 3 offers insight into these and more questions about the fact and fiction of gifted readers.

REFLECT

Once you identify your gifted readers, consider if and how you may already be providing them with literacy instruction beyond foundational skills.

REFERENCES

Brett, A., Rothlein, L., & Hurley, M. (1996). Vocabulary acquisition from listening to stories and explanations of target words. *Elementary School Journal, 96*(4), 415–422.

Foorman, B., Francis, D., Fletcher, J., Schatschneider, C., & Mehta, P. (1998). The role of instruction in learning to read: Preventing reading failure in at-risk children. *Journal of Educational Psychology, 90*(1), 37–55.

Jackson, N. E. (1993). *Reading with young children* (RBDM 9302). Storrs, CT: National Research Center on the Gifted and Talented, University of Connecticut.

Knight, B. A. (2001, July). *Keynote address: Enabling the poppies to bloom.* Queensland Regional Gifted and Talented Conference, Rockhampton, Australia.

National Institute of Child Health and Human Development (NICHD). (2000). Report of the National Reading Panel: Teaching children to read: An evidence-based assessment of the scientific research literature on reading and its implications for reading instruction: Reports of the subgroups (NIH Publication No. 00-4754). Washington, DC: US Government Printing Office.

National Assessment of Educational Progress (NAEP). (2017). *NAEP reading report card* (NCES publication). Washington, DC: US Government Printing Office. Retrieved from https://www.nationsreportcard.gov/reading_2017/#?grade=4

Wood, P. F. (2008). Reading instruction with gifted and talented readers: A series of unfortunate events or a sequence of auspicious results? *Gifted Child Today, 31*(3), 16–24.

Chapter Three

Fact or Fiction About Gifted Readers

"Know your kids, and know your books."—Bob Seney

SCENARIO

Mr. Guercia groans, a common reaction around the teacher tables during this in-service data workshop. The results of the state tests were in, and as he surveys the page from his third-grade class, he runs his yellow highlighter down the list, identifying the reading scores of his lowest 25%. There are three fewer students in the below-level category this year than last. With a sigh of relief, Mr. Guercia sees the proverbial needle finally move in the right direction. He must be doing something right. This confirms what he believes to be true: Provide appropriate interventions, and students will improve. They will make progress.

The assistant principal, Ms. Fairweather, doesn't want to burst anyone's bubble about the progress their students made in the most recent administration of the state reading test. Their progress, although exciting to see, is not the end of the story. Her teachers had more work to do—just not in the area in which they were accustomed.

Fairweather applauded her teachers' efforts: "We've done a great job working with our strugglers. We've spent a lot of time, energy, and resources equipping both teachers and students for the challenge of getting our kids all up to grade level in reading. Over the past five years we have seen incremental growth that is finally culminating in adequate progress for these kiddos.

"There's just one thing: Our lowest 25% is not the only group who needs to show progress. Our readers in this school range from below the 10th percentile to above the 90th percentile. That's a wide range of reading achievement in a very diverse school like ours. We are required to enable all

17

students to make continuous progress in reading. Unfortunately, this means we have fallen short. Our gifted and advanced readers are not making progress," Fairweather explains. "Time to roll up our sleeves and redouble our efforts for all of our kids." As a call to arms, Fairweather's speech (or appeal) falls flat with the faculty.

Mr. Guercia groans again, louder than before. "We don't have to worry about those above the 90th percentile. They're already at or above grade level. And there are so few of them, so it really won't make a difference in our scores," Guercia complains. "I'm already overwhelmed with those who struggle. I don't see how I can focus on those who don't struggle, too."

"Then we have a problem," Fairweather says. *And we have a lot of work to do*, she thinks.

The Every Student Succeeds Act (ESSA) of 2015 includes two new requirements that affect how we work with gifted learners. First, on state report cards, states must include student achievement data at each achievement level that is disaggregated by student subgroup. In the past, states provided detailed information for students performing at the proficient level and below. Now, states must also include information on students achieving at the advanced level.

The second requirement under ESSA provides that, when states apply for Title II professional development funds, they must include information about how they plan to improve the skills of teachers and other school leaders that will enable them to identify gifted and talented students and provide instruction based on their students' needs. Both of these 2015 ESSA requirements support the facts about gifted readers and their needs. In order to meet these requirements, districts and schools need to dispel any lingering myths about these students and support the dissemination of the facts instead.

LET'S LOOK AT THE FACTS

What we know about gifted readers may not be based in fact. It may instead be based on myths about gifted learners in general. We need to separate the fact from the fiction about gifted readers before we can learn how to differentiate our reading instruction for them. There are four myths that, once debunked, provide the space to plan effective literacy instruction for gifted and accelerated readers. Consider the following quiz to see which myths operate freely within your institution.[1]

1. Gifted and talented readers as a group are homogeneous and should receive the same reading instruction.

a. True
b. False
c. Sometimes

2. Gifted and talented readers seek out challenging or more advanced reading materials on their own.

a. True
b. False
c. Sometimes

3. Gifted and talented readers are experts at text comprehension.

a. True
b. False
c. Sometimes

4. Gifted and talented readers should be given complete control over their choice of reading materials.

a. True
b. False
c. Sometimes

Part of any learning process in which new information must be incorporated is to link it to prior knowledge. What teachers believe is true about the students they serve often translates into the actions they take on behalf of those same students. Believing these myths means that no action will be taken by teachers to differentiate literacy instruction for gifted and accelerated readers. Once these myths are debunked, a new set of beliefs or facts should encourage new actions, as well. Each of these facts about gifted readers provides teachers with insight into how to plan for and teach them.

Fact 1: Gifted and Talented Readers as a Group Are Heterogeneous and Require Specially Designed Instruction.

In order to plan effective literacy instruction for gifted readers, it's important to understand our readers: who they are, the skills they already possess, and their reading preferences. Gifted and talented readers, as a group, differ in these three areas. They may all be fluent readers, but they will differ in the areas of background, skill, and interest. Providing a positive and robust reading culture (Seney, 2017) can capture the attention and imaginations of this varied group of gifted readers.

sitive and robust reading culture includes the use of specially de-
struction (SDI). SDI is defined by IDEA (2004) as

> adapting, as appropriate to the needs of an eligible child, the content, metho-
> dology, or delivery of instruction to address the unique needs of the child that
> result from the child's exceptionality and to ensure access of the child to the
> general curriculum, so that the child can meet the educational standards within
> the jurisdiction of the public agency that apply to all children.

When applied to the identified needs of gifted students, SDI means the following:

- Appropriate instruction is based on the individual student's need and ability.
- The rate, level, and manner of instruction should benefit the student in a
  meaningful way.
- Instruction should go beyond the general education program through enrichment, acceleration, or both.

Gifted readers require modification in content, process, product, or a combination of these, along with complexity and rigor. The use of SDI, based on
gifted students' needs, creates the positive culture. The addition of a complex
and rigorous reading curriculum makes the culture robust. Some suggestions
that nurture a positive and robust reading culture include the following:

- Use basic skill and content area curriculum compacting.
- Investigate real problems through inquiry reading.
- Provide students with reading choices with clearly defined outcomes.
- Use a variety of grouping, such as cluster, flexible, and ability, to differen-
  tiate reading instruction.
- Identify a student's interest for targeted reading to learn.

Fact 2: Gifted and Talented Readers Should Be Encouraged to Seek Out Challenging or More Advanced Reading Materials.

When not challenged, gifted readers may and often do become complacent
readers. Although they are typically characterized as voracious and early
readers with large vocabularies, they may not be reading beyond their independent reading level. The independent reading level is the highest level of
reading a child does without help. The independent reading level is not
challenging to a gifted reader. Reis and Boeve (2009) propose that gifted
readers need to engage in a "supported struggle" in reading so that they can
learn more complex and in-depth material than they would otherwise without
support.

How might teachers encourage gifted readers to seek out those challenges and engage in that supported struggle? Matching the reader to text is not a new idea. Allington (2002) recommends this approach for struggling readers, but this approach promises to make a difference for all readers, including gifted readers. Educators can focus on matching both the reading level of text to readers and reader interests to text. Research suggests that readers who make their own text choices based on their interests enjoy reading more (Reis et al., 2004). If teachers look for reading opportunities that marry level with interests, then gifted readers can be challenged.

Fact 3: Gifted and Talented Readers May Be Fluent Readers but Are Not Always Critical Readers.

One of the differences between average readers and gifted readers is gifted readers' above-average ability to read fluently with comprehension. For many gifted readers, reading is considered a preferred activity, and they will read with persistence in areas of great interest to them. However, although often characterized as voracious readers, gifted readers may not always be critical readers. In order to move readers beyond the confines of a basal reader, which emphasizes decoding and vocabulary, teachers can provide guidance around what types of literature are appropriate and challenging for gifted readers.

In order to support gifted readers to become more critical readers, teachers can facilitate shifts in reading instruction. Consider replacing any basal texts with literature. Model critical thinking by using higher-level questioning techniques. Facilitate discussion around texts through a Socratic or shared-inquiry model. Focus on analysis and evaluation levels of learning (Vosslamber, 2002) in response to text experiences. Teach readers how to evaluate literature on its merits. The teacher as facilitator can add the depth and complexity needed for gifted readers.

Learn more about fostering critical reading for gifted readers in chapter six.

Fact 4: Gifted and Talented Readers Need Guidance Over Their Choice of Reading Materials.

Although gifted and advanced readers have the potential to read beyond their age range and their independent reading level, they often stick close to their comfort zones of familiar genres and topics of nonfiction texts. They need guidance in the selection of their reading materials. Both teachers and parents can offer this guidance. For a gifted reader to grow, a combination of enrichment and acceleration opportunities in the area of reading materials can be used. Because there are individual differences between gifted readers, reading material should be selected according to their individual needs (Hartley, 1996).

Gifted readers need guidance over their choice of reading materials based on their identified cognitive needs. Teachers can guide gifted readers to texts that meet these cognitive needs. Clark (1983) provides a list of cognitive needs that differentiate gifted readers from typical readers. Gifted learners need

- to be exposed to new and challenging information about the environment and the culture,
- to be exposed to varied subjects and concerns,
- to be allowed to pursue ideas as far as their interests take them,
- to encounter and use increasingly difficult vocabulary and concepts, and
- to pursue inquiries beyond allotted time spans.

SOME SUGGESTIONS TO REACH AND TEACH GIFTED READERS BASED ON THE FACTS

As teachers consider the facts about gifted readers, recommended best practices for both elementary and secondary gifted readers can be applied that will contribute to a positive reading culture. The tips in Table 3.1 are categorized by grade level, but they are not exclusive to that grade level. Tips listed here emphasize practices that may be underused or forgotten at that level.

CONCLUSION

Dispelling the myths about gifted readers and embracing the facts is a first step in providing gifted readers with a challenging reading program that will support positive outcomes for them. Ideally, the shift from learning to read to reading to learn should occur in the early grades, but that may not be the experience gifted readers have had prior to entering middle or high school. This shift must occur and should occur sooner rather than later if we are to keep gifted readers engaged.

* * *

From the Expert

Dr. Bob Seney, professor emeritus of gifted studies: "Fostering gifted readers to become skilled, passionate, habitual, and critical readers"

When I have the chance, I like to visit classrooms and talk to students to see what they are reading and what they like and simply to listen to them. In

Table 3.1. Tips for Teaching Gifted Readers

Elementary Gifted Readers	Secondary Gifted Readers
• Replace the basal reader or whole-class reading program materials with chapter books and literature. • Use an interest inventory, such as the Interest-A-Lyzer (Renzulli, 1997), to determine gifted readers' points of interest. • Compact reading curriculum in order to expose gifted readers to more advanced content and products. • Use instructional (ability) grouping to enable students to read more advanced texts in their areas of interest. • Assess students' comprehension using higher-order questions. • Provide texts that are adequately challenging.	• Create a culture of reading in your class or school (Seney, 2017). • Read aloud to students. • Have books ever present (multiple copies of the same title). • Allow students to select their own reading materials. • Provide opportunities for students to share what they are reading, both formally and informally. • Facilitate book discussions through Socratic seminars or shared inquiry. • Have students set their own reading goals. • Provide gifted readers with tasks that have more complex resources, research, issues, problems, skills, or goals.

conversations with gifted readers over several visits—over several years—I have found that I was hearing very much the same thing. I was hearing:

1. "The books that we are assigned to read do not match my interests."
2. "The books that we read do not relate to me or my life."
3. "The books that we read are not challenging."
4. "I have read the books before, sometimes several years ago."
5. "Nobody seems to know the new and good books to read."
6. "I don't know where to go to find out about new books."

This suggests that we have some work to do, and it has led me to create what I now call my mantra: "Know the reader, know the literature, and make the match!" A good reference here is Lesesne (2003).

We have to remember that many, if not most, gifted students are early and sophisticated readers and they have developed reading tastes, preferences, and favorite genres at an early age. Too often, they surpass the reading experience of their teachers or are forced into reading instruction programs of which they have no need. I have often said that reading instruction for the gifted should be based on reading to learn and not learning to read. So, this is a problem that *we* have created.

We have not listened to our gifted and advanced readers. We must come to know them. To know our readers, simply talk to them in informal or even formal interviews; have the students complete interest inventories; watch what they pick up and read—listen to what they recommend to other students. In other words, do some careful observation of your students.

In knowing the literature, Stephen Layne (2009) has a great chapter in his book *Igniting a Passion for Reading: Successful Strategies for Building Lifetime Readers* called "I Didn't Know They Still Wrote Books for Adults" (chapter 3). Teachers must read the latest in children's and young adult literature. However, these two markets are really hot right now, and the marketplace is flooded with new and great books. You must create partnerships with other teachers and most importantly with librarians!

I know of schools where teachers have formed book clubs in which they read exclusively children's and young adult literature and share with each other. Layne (2009) also suggests creating a First Readers Club with your librarian. When new books come into the library, these students have the first choice to read the books and then to make comments, recommendations, and so on that are posted and shared. These students are recognized by placing a label in the book with their names listed as a First Reader. Great idea! Kids like recommendations from other kids.

Over the years, I have read extensively in children's and young adult literature, and I select literature following Judith Halsted's criteria of books most suitable for gifted readers, which I share extensively—literally all over the world. We have to work together, but a good starting place for an individual is to look at quality award lists. In the United States, the American Library Association's Newbery, Caldecott, and Printz Award lists are great resources.

Unfortunately, I see little being done to make reading programs appropriate for gifted readers at any level. Call it differentiating for gifted readers if you want, but make reading and reading programs appropriate to meet their needs, to speak to their interests, and to provide appropriate challenges. Current research strongly suggests that self-selecting reading material is very important. Often, we don't give these readers enough credit.

While the classics are important, I think that depending on the classics as the basis of reading selections is a mistake. These great books from another time, another place, another mind-set, and another system of vocabulary and syntax simply do not speak to the contemporary reader. At this time, one of our first tasks is to hook reluctant readers back into involved reading. Assigning the classics simply won't work and will in fact turn readers not only off the classics but off reading, as well. There is research that supports this.

This is why I strongly encourage teachers, especially secondary teachers, to use young adult literature in the classroom. Contemporary YA literature has come of age. It demonstrates the same skillful craftsmanship employed in all good literature, and it translates to the world of young adults the same conflicts and issues with which all humans struggle (Monseau & Salvner, 1992).

I especially like a quote from Robert Probst (1988) about the impo
of young adult literature:

> Young adult literature in the classroom is important because it ". . . strikes at
> issues that matter to the students, issues with which they are grappling in their
> own private lives. It has the power to stimulate the kind of creative involved
> reading that transforms text into literature. Because it deals with events, situa-
> tions, and emotions that they may share or understand. It vests them with
> authority as reader—authority that they may lack when they confront more
> complex texts and thus encourages them to assume the responsibility of mak-
> ing sense for themselves, of texts, and therefore of their own conceptions of
> the world.

At almost every presentation I do, I say, "Our goal is to help every single
reader, especially gifted readers, to become skilled, passionate, habitual, and
critical readers." If we do not provide the guidance, the support, the nurturing
to these readers, what will we have lost? And I am not just thinking of the
world of literature here. Every human endeavor depends on skilled, analytic
readers. We must provide appropriate, interesting, and challenging literature,
both fiction and nonfiction, to help these readers move to a deeper level.
When we do this, we create lifelong readers in both their personal reading
and their professional reading. Surely, this is what we want as teachers!

If you're not sure what to do first with your gifted readers, I think maybe
what we must do is just get out of their way! Our task in encouraging gifted
readers is to provide the resources; a supporting environment; a strong example in our own personal reading; and, importantly, opportunities for them to
share and discuss what they are reading with you, the teacher, and their peers.

One of the richest experiences that I had as a middle school teacher was to
schedule regular student-led reading conferences. Not only did I hear some
absolutely remarkable reactions and analysis of literature, but I also created
positive teacher-student relationships, which translated to a powerful and
positive classroom environment. These conferences also led to writing conferences, which is an important area we have not addressed. There is and
must be a reading-writing connection.

* * *

ASSIGNMENT: BEYOND THE BASAL:
LET'S READ 100 GREAT BOOKS!

Replace your basal readers with the list of 100 great books every young adult
should read. Create a group within the Goodreads platform (https://
goodreads.com). As students read a book, have them monitor their progress,

create a Goodreads profile for it, and then review it. Within the Goodreads platform, students can rate the book, engage in a discussion about the book, and recommend it to others. By the end of the school year, your class will have an archive of all of the books they have read and related to.

REFLECT

How comfortable are you with allowing gifted readers to make their own choices based on their own preferences for books? Are you ready to let go of that control?

NOTE

1. The answers to the quiz are (1) b, (2) b, (3) b, (4) c.

REFERENCES

Allington, Richard. (2002). What I've learned about effective reading instruction: From a decade of studying exemplary elementary classroom teachers. *Phi Delta Kappan.* 83. 740–747. 10.1177/003172170208301007.

Clark, B. (1983). *Growing up gifted.* Columbus, OH: Merrill.

Halsted, J. W. (2002). *Some of my best friends are books: Guiding gifted readers from preschool to high school.* Goshen, KY: Great Potential Press.

Hartley, M. (1996). Reading and literature. In D. McAlpine & R. Moltzen (Eds.), *Gifted and talented: New Zealand perspective*s (pp. 253–272). Palmerston North, New Zealand: Educational Research and Development Center, Massey University.

Individuals With Disabilities Act (IDEA), 34 CFR §300.39(b)(3) (2004).

Layne, S. L. (2009). *Igniting a passion for reading: Successful strategies for building lifetime readers.* Portland, ME: Stenhouse.

Lesesne, T. (2003). *Making the match.* Portland, ME: Stenhouse.

Monseau, Virginia R., & Salvner, Gary M. *Reading their world: The young adult novel in the classroom.* Portsmouth, NH: Boynton/Cook, 1992.

Probst, R. (1988). *Response and analysis: Teaching literature in junior and senior high school.* Portsmouth, NH: Boynton, Cook.

Reis, S. M., & Boeve, H. (2009). How academically gifted elementary, urban students respond to challenge in an enriched, differentiated reading program. *Journal for the Education of the Gifted, 33*(2), 203–240. Retrieved from https://doi.org/10.1177/016235320903300204

Reis, S. M., Gubbins, E. J., Briggs, C. J., Schreiber, F. J., Richards, S., & Jacobs, J. K. (2004). Reading instruction for talented readers: Case studies documenting few opportunities for continuous progress. *Gifted Child Quarterly, 48,* 315–338.

Renzulli, J. (1997). *Interest-a-lyzer family of instruments: A manual for teachers.* Waco, TX: Prufrock Press.

Seney, R. W. (2017, July 20–23). *Reading and the gifted: Developing a program of reading with a global perspective.* World Conference for Gifted and Talented Children, Sydney, New South Wales, Australia.

Vosslamber, A. (2002, Spring). Gifted readers: Who are they, and how can they be served in the classroom? *Gifted Child Today Magazine.* Retrieved from http://www.casenex.com/casenet/pages/virtualLibrary/mlandrum/giftedreader.htm

Chapter Four

Characteristics of Gifted Readers

"Hide not your talents. They for use were made. What's a sundial in the shade?"—Benjamin Franklin

SCENARIO

Marla's two sons have been identified as gifted by their public school system. They are both in gifted enrichment classes one day a week at their local elementary school. They are both keenly interested in a variety of topics and dive headfirst into the depths of learning all about them. They are quite alike except in one area: reading.

Nicholas taught himself to read at age 3 and propelled himself to a fifth-grade reading level by kindergarten. Collin learned to read through phonics instruction with extra help on a more average timeline. By first grade, he is reading on a second-grade level. Although Collin is still reading above grade level, he has no interest in reading. He does not read for pleasure. Nicholas, on the other hand, reads voraciously for both information and pleasure.

Marla thinks that the Reading Counts Program at their school might encourage both of her boys to read texts that are more complex and will meet their advanced reading needs. Unfortunately, Nicholas is bored by the confines of the program, and Collin reacts negatively to the competitive elements of the program and refuses to participate. The summer reading experience Marla set up for her boys at the local library likewise does not inspire. Completing the prescribed reading list within two weeks in order to win a prize easily broken and easily forgotten does not engage or move ahead either Nicholas or Collin.

Underachievement lurks when gifted students are not engaged in learning. By the time Nicholas is in fourth grade and Collin is in third, their paths diverge even wider. Collin flourishes in a more traditional approach to reading instruction when it is set at his grade level. Nicholas, whose hunger for more advanced and complex texts goes unsatisfied, begins to shut down. He begins to experience daily stomachaches and does not want to go to school. Marla knows that Nicholas needs more than he is getting during reading instruction.

Well-versed in the nature and needs of her gifted children, she approaches the teachers and the principal with both her concerns and some research-based approaches to help her son. After a marathon-like conference discussing the merits of acceleration, advanced groupings, curriculum compacting, and even allowing Nicholas to pursue an independent project of interest, the principal tells Marla something no parent wants to hear: "I can't get my teachers to do what they don't want to do. I guess we can't help you here."

Stunned, Marla makes a decision few parents are willing to make. She pulls her son from the neighborhood elementary school and homeschools him for the next four years. Although both Nicholas and Collin are gifted students, Nicholas is a gifted reader. His needs require so much more than Marla had anticipated.

THE UNIQUE NEEDS OF GIFTED READERS

A host of characteristics of gifted learners intersect with the process of reading. Although there are a variety of ways in which gifted students are defined and identified, it's important to first summarize some of the most common indicators. The National Association for Gifted Children (NAGC, 2010a) defines *giftedness* as

> individuals . . . who demonstrate outstanding levels of aptitude (defined as an exceptional ability to reason and learn) or competence (documented performance or achievement in top 10% or rarer) in one or more domains. Domains include any structured area of activity with its own symbol system (e.g., mathematics, music, language) and/or set of sensorimotor skills (e.g., painting, dance, sports). (para. 1)

When you seek to define gifted readers, you must first connect their characteristics to the definition of *reading*. According to Adams and Brock (1993), *reading* is the ability to comprehend the message that the author intended based on accurate decoding.

THE GIFTED READER

Although different theories offer lists of characteristics that can be applied to the gifted reader, taking a broader themes approach is more appropriate than a discrete list. Sally Reis and her colleagues (2005) at the University of Connecticut have identified several broad themes about gifted and talented readers.

Gifted readers are most often characterized by reading early and at advanced levels. This is the most recognizable and most commonly observed characteristic. It is measurable and the one that parents and teachers, even those without prior experience with gifted children, can point to and say, "This child is gifted!" It's important to consider, however, that not all gifted children are gifted readers, so if this characteristic is not observed in a child, it does not mean they are not gifted.

Gifted readers use advanced processing in reading. This means they use advanced reading strategies to unlock text meaning. Expert use of both syntactic and semantic processes defines the gifted reader. They use context naturally to aid comprehension and avail themselves to the role syntax plays in coherent sentences. Gifted readers go well beyond word recognition to make meaning; they use context to support both word recognition and text meaning much like an adult would (Schwantes, 1991).

Gifted readers read with enthusiasm and enjoyment. Parents and teachers often agree that—metaphorically speaking—gifted readers *inhale books.* They read with gusto, and books become their constant companions. Judith Wynn Halsted (2009) poses that gifted readers often intensely identify with characters in books; they process their social and emotional skills through reading. The complex connections gifted readers make to the characters and plots drive a continuous cycle of enthusiasm for reading and pleasure in the activity. Reading for enjoyment is in addition to reading for information for gifted readers. As a result of this enthusiasm, they develop their own reading preferences and favorite genres at an early age. A great way to get to know the child is to know what books they love.

Gifted readers demonstrate advanced language skills (oral, reading, and written). Gifted readers are advanced in linguistic abilities; they read with high levels of fluency (accuracy, rate, and expression) and layered comprehension. By definition, they may be highly verbal and process their comprehension with ease through discussion and dialogue. They may also excel in creative writing or literary analysis (Wood, 2008). This characteristic, more than the others, is what leads teachers to conclude that gifted readers do not require any reading instruction.

Gifted readers display higher levels of self-regulation than do other students. Gifted readers often exhibit high levels of task commitment to the activity of reading (Reis et al., 2005). When gifted readers are enthusiastic and their purpose for reading is based on interest, they display greater use of cognitive and metacognitive strategies, such as planning, self-monitoring, and focusing while reading (Housand & Reis, 2008). These are self-regulation skills that often must be explicitly taught to typical readers and learners.

Self-regulation activities like keeping track of what they've read, being intentional in their book selection, and setting goals for themselves in reading, set the gifted reader apart from typical readers.

SO, WHAT DO GIFTED READERS NEED?

The aforementioned characteristics, in combination with the assertion that gifted readers do not need to learn to read but instead read to learn, reveal the following educational needs. Gifted readers need

- experiences with text that go beyond the basal or leveled reader,
- instruction that focuses on their strengths and interests (Reis & Renzulli, 2014),
- to be allowed to pursue their interests and ideas in depth (Levande, 1999),
- opportunities to respond to and interact with others about a text (Seney, 2017), and
- reading instruction that facilitates critical and creative reading (Levande, 1999).

These are some of the tenets of differentiation for the gifted reader. When reading instruction is too easy, there is a danger of gifted readers becoming lazy or complacent learners. The appropriate match between the reader's ability, interests, and strengths makes for efficient and forward-moving learning. Chall and Conrad (1991) equate this match as being slightly above the reader's independent level, normally referred to as the instructional level. Gifted readers require reading instruction at their instructional level the same as every reader.

HOW CAN WE MEET THESE EDUCATIONAL NEEDS?

Once the educational needs of gifted readers are identified and defined, they can be targeted with appropriate instruction. The nature of the differentiation for gifted readers focuses primarily on depth and complexity. Learning to ask and respond to higher-level questions helps gifted readers meet their own needs. Kaplan's (1994) Depth and Complexity Framework (DCF) helps students go beyond a basic understanding of a topic and facilitates critical and creative thinking.

The DCF employs 11 icons that trigger students to first contextualize their learning and then to ask and seek answers to higher-level questions (see Table 4.1). The teacher as facilitator, not director, leads readers through a reading journey that is deep and wide.

The Depth and Complexity Framework, applied to reading ir
works well at both the elementary and secondary levels. Conside
take readers through a literary or informational text on a deep dive to e̶n̶c̶o̶u̶n̶
ter more complex comprehension questions. Each icon in the DCF triggers a
different level of comprehension questions. Consider the reading prompts
connected to each DCF icon as you plan reading instruction for gifted readers.

Name and Icon	Reading Prompts
Language of the Discipline	• Does the author use figurative language? Where? • Does the author use certain words or language (e.g., science, history, veterinary medicine)? • Does the use of particular words tell you where the story takes place (e.g., pueblo, ranch, underground, freshwater habitat)? • What products are made? • What methods are used? • What special writing technique does the author use?
Details	• Who, what, when, where, why? (Retell) • Compare and contrast [characters, scenes, actions, topics]. • What are the physical features of a character? • What traits does a character have? • What are the text's attributes? • What details define [a topic; e.g., spiders]? • How are the pictures important to the story?
Patterns	• Are there any events, words, or phrases that repeat? Why? What is the significance of this? • Retell the main sequence of events. • What predictions can you make based on a character's actions so far? • Discuss the patterns that exist in different genres. • Is there a life cycle? • Discuss one cause-and-effect relationship from the story.
Unanswered Questions	• What is still uncertain? • Does reading about this topic bring up more questions? • Unfamiliar vocabulary—what words don't you understand? • KWL: What do you know, what do you want to know, and what have you learned? • Can you infer the setting of the story based on the clues? • Can you infer why a character acted the way he or she did based on the clues?

Table 4.1. Reading Prompts Using DCF. Adapted from Silver Creek Elementary School (2019).

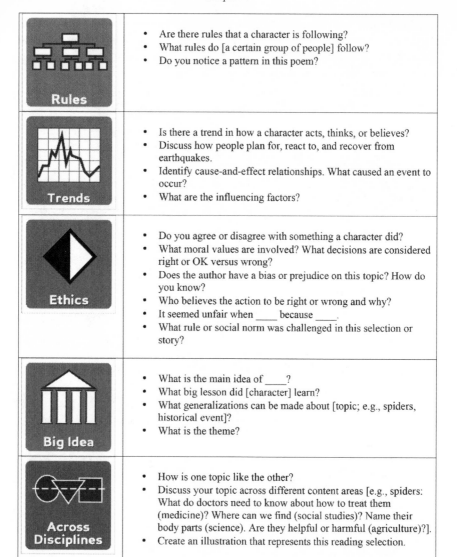

Rules	• Are there rules that a character is following? • What rules do [a certain group of people] follow? • Do you notice a pattern in this poem?
Trends	• Is there a trend in how a character acts, thinks, or believes? • Discuss how people plan for, react to, and recover from earthquakes. • Identify cause-and-effect relationships. What caused an event to occur? • What are the influencing factors?
Ethics	• Do you agree or disagree with something a character did? • What moral values are involved? What decisions are considered right or OK versus wrong? • Does the author have a bias or prejudice on this topic? How do you know? • Who believes the action to be right or wrong and why? • It seemed unfair when ____ because ____. • What rule or social norm was challenged in this selection or story?
Big Idea	• What is the main idea of ____? • What big lesson did [character] learn? • What generalizations can be made about [topic; e.g., spiders, historical event]? • What is the theme?
Across Disciplines	• How is one topic like the other? • Discuss your topic across different content areas [e.g., spiders: What do doctors need to know about how to treat them (medicine)? Where can we find (social studies)? Name their body parts (science). Are they helpful or harmful (agriculture)?]. • Create an illustration that represents this reading selection.

Table 4.1. Reading Prompts Using DCF. Adapted from Silver Creek Elementary School (2019) (cont'd).

 Over Time	• How did a character change from the beginning of the book to the end? What made that happen? • Is there a change in setting? Is this important to the events in the story? • Examine how a character learns a lesson. • Discuss how the actions of the past influence what occurs now. • How has [topic] changed over time? • How have your opinions or feelings changed after reading this text or studying this topic?
 Multiple Perspectives	• How does each character's point of view affect the actions they take? • Does one character's point of view influence what another character does in the story or the problem? • What are the two opposing views on this issue? • Would a [profession; e.g., scientist] see this same topic the same way? Why? • Who disagrees or agrees? • What are their opinions? Why? • Another way to solve the problem is ____.

Table 4.1. Reading Prompts Using DCF. Adapted from Silver Creek Elementary School (2019) (cont'd).

Each unit or lesson during reading instruction or an English language arts class can be differentiated in a way to meet the educational needs of gifted readers by framing materials, instruction, and activities through the lens of depth and complexity. Table 4.1 prompts teachers to think deeply so that, in turn, they will facilitate that deep learning for their students.

Choice and Variety of Learning Materials

Building on the strategy of providing choice to gifted readers, provide opportunities for open-ended, self-directed reading activities. Use advanced supplementary materials that foster the read-to-learn mind-set of gifted readers. One approach to this type of differentiation is to use a Think-Tac-Toe choice chart (see Table 4.2). Based on the work of the Multiple Menu Model (Renzulli, Leppien, & Hays, 2000), create ways for gifted readers to engage with text on a variety of levels through a variety of ways and to be able to share what they've learned in a variety of expressions.

Consider a Think-Tac-Toe for a novel. Provide students with these directions: *Select and complete one activity from each horizontal row to help you and others think about your novel. Remember to make your work thoughtful, original, rich with detail, and accurate.*

Table 4.2. Think-Tac-Toe

Create a pair of collages that compare you and a character in the book. Compare and contrast physical and personality traits. Label your collages so viewers understand your thinking.	Write a bio-poem about yourself and another about a main character in the book so your readers see how you and the character are alike and different. Be sure to include the most important traits in each poem.	Write a recipe or set of directions for how you would solve a problem and another for how a main character in the book would solve a problem. Your list should help us know you and the character.
Draw or paint and write a greeting card that invites us into the scenery and mood of an important part of the book. Be sure the verse helps us understand what is important in the scene and why.	Make a model or a map of a key place in your life and an important one from the novel. Find a way to help viewers understand both what the places are like and why they are important in your life and the characters' lives.	Make two timelines. The first should illustrate and describe at least six to eight shifts in settings in the book. The second should explain and illustrate how the mood changes with changes in setting.
Using books of proverbs, quotations, or both, find at least six to eight that you feel reflect what's important about the novel's theme. Find at least six to eight that do the same for your life. Display them, and explain your choices.	Interview a key character from the book to find out what lessons he or she thinks we should learn from events in the book.	Find several songs you think reflect an important message from the book. Prepare an audio collage. Write an exhibit card that helps your listener understand how you think these songs express the book's meaning.

CONCLUSION

Appropriate reading instruction for gifted readers happens at the intersection of the characteristics of the gifted reader and their educational needs. As Bob Seney regularly expresses in his mantra "Know the reader, know the literature, and make the match," without knowing the reader, you cannot make appropriate instructional choices.

ACTIVITY: BOOK TALKS

Time to go beyond the book report and tap into the gifted reader's love for books. If books are your best friends, then introducing those friends to others is a natural next step. The book talk is a perfect opportunity to explore depth and complexity with gifted readers by exploring, developing, and researching an area of interest (NAGC, 2010b). The following is a more traditional approach to a book talk. How students share their book talks should be up to

them. Give them choice of expression. Following this traditiona
are suggestions to expand the book talk in both critical and creative

Encourage students to take their book talks to the next level
more depth and complexity options. Erika Saunders (2019), a middle school
teacher of the gifted, offers the following ideas:

- Create a 30-second movie commercial or trailer podcast.
- Design a room that a character would have.
- Make a new book cover with a write-up and short pitch on why this should
  be the new cover.
- Turn the book into a short play.
- Create a fan blog.
- Design a movie poster.
- Write a letter to the head of a production company convincing them to
  make a movie.
- Write a letter to the fan club of the book.
- Create an interview with the author.
- Be a talk-show host interviewing the author.
- Rewrite the story using a new setting.
- Tell the story through a different character. Dress up like the character and
  retell the story. Write a summary from that character's point of view.
- Be a costume designer for the movie version.
- Be a set designer for the movie version.
- Create a graphic novel version of the book.
- Create your own summary of what you think the sequel should be.
- Create a rap or song summary.
- Create a TV show theme song.
- Illustrate the book.
- Make a documentary.
- Be a newscaster reporting the story.
- Make an audition video for a part in the movie version.
- Record a voiceover.
- Describe the conflict or problem as a sportscast.
- Create a *Jeopardy!* game based on the book.
- Cast the movie or TV show version.
- Link a real social or societal problem that relates to the story.
- Create a theme list, and include books that fit into the theme.
- Create a photo album based on the book.
- Create a magazine based on the book.
- Write an advice column for the characters.
- Be the author's editor. Change one part to make the book better.
- Rewrite the book as a children's book.

ASSIGNMENT: READABILITY ROUND-UP

In order to make the best match possible between the reader and text, first do a readability study of both. What you learn will help you better guide readers to their perfect match.

For this assignment, please identify your gifted readers and consider their reading ability; cultural, ethnic, or linguistic backgrounds; and other defining characteristics (e.g., gender, socioeconomic status).

Share insights you've gained about your students' backgrounds, current strengths, and areas of challenge in reading (e.g., word recognition, comprehension, fluency). Then, fill out Table 4.3 for each student. What do you notice about the match between books and readers?

This is the most important component of your readability assignment. This is where you pull together connections about the importance of readability levels and how leveling systems can provide a tool to help you provide effective literacy intervention or instruction. In your narrative, explore the following questions:

- What do you notice about the match between your students and the books they find interesting or are reading for class?
- Does the purpose for reading make a difference?
- Does the type of text (genre) play a role?
- Do your students seem to be reading at an independent, instructional, or frustration level for most classroom tasks?
- What insights might you gain from understanding your students' reading levels and the readability levels of various required and self-selected texts?

REFLECT

Are you paying attention to what your students are reading? Who decides what goes home in their book bags? Do your gifted readers have access to more advanced texts?

Table 4.3. Current and Recent Reads for Students

Title	Readability Level
1. _____	1. _____
2. _____	2. _____
3. _____	3. _____

REFERENCES

Adams, M. (1990). *Beginning to read: Thinking and learning about print*. Cambridge, MA: MIT Press.

Chall, J. S., & Conrad, S. S. (1991). *Should textbooks challenge students? The case for easier or harder textbooks*. New York: Teachers College Press.

Halsted, J. W. (2009). *Some of my best friends are books: Guiding gifted readers from pre-school to high school*. Tucson, AZ: Great Potential Press.

Housand, A., & Reis, S. M. (2008, November). Self-regulated learning in reading: Gifted pedagogy and instructional settings. *Journal of Advanced Academics, 20*(1), 108–136.

Kaplan, S. (1994). *Differentiating the core curriculum and instruction to provide advanced learning opportunities*. Sacramento: California Department of Education and California Association for the Gifted.

Levande, D. (1999). Gifted readers and reading instruction. *CAG Communicator, 30*(1). Retrieved from http://hoagiesgifted.org/levande

National Association for Gifted Children (NAGC). (2010a). *Position statement: Redefining giftedness for a new century: Shifting the paradigm*. Retrieved from https://www.dvusd.org/cms/lib/AZ01901092/Centricity/Domain/95/Definitions%20of%20Giftedness.pdf

National Association for Gifted Children (NAGC). (2010b, November). *NAGC Pre-K–Grade 12 Gifted Programming Standards: A Blueprint for Quality Gifted Education Programs*. Washington, DC: Author. Retrieved from http://www.nagc.org/sites/default/files/standards/K-12%20standards%20booklet.pdf

Reis, S. M., Eckert, R. D., Schreiber, F. J., Jacobs, J., Briggs, C., Gubbins, E. J., Coyne, M., & Muller, L. (2005, September). *The schoolwide enrichment model reading study* (RM05214). Storrs: University of Connecticut, the National Research Center on the Gifted and Talented. Retrieved from https://nrcgt.uconn.edu/wp-content/uploads/sites/953/2015/04/rm05214.pdf

Reis, S. M., & Renzulli, J. (2014). *The schoolwide enrichment model: A how-to guide for talent development* (3rd ed.). Waco, TX: Prufrock Press.

Renzulli, J. S., Leppien, J. H., & Hays, T. S. (2000). *The multiple menu model: A practical guide for developing differentiated curriculum*. Mansfield Center, CT: Creative Learning Press.

Saunders, E. (2019). Beyond the book report. *Byrdseed*. Retrieved from https://www.byrdseed.com/41-ways-to-go-beyond-the-book-report/

Schwantes, F. M. (1991). Children's use of semantic and syntactic information for word recognition and determination of sentence meaningfulness. *Journal of Reading Behavior, 23*(3), 335–250. Retrieved from https://journals.sagepub.com/doi/pdf/10.1080/10862969109547745

Seney, R. W. (2017, July 20–23). *Reading and the gifted: Developing a program of reading with a global perspective*. World Conference for Gifted and Talented Children, Sydney, New South Wales, Australia.

Silver Creek Elementary School. (2019). *Reading comprehension: Depth and complexity*. Adams 12 School District, Colorado. Retrieved from https://silvercreek.adams12.org/sites/silvercreek.d7sb.adams12.org/files/attachments/ReadingPromptsDepthComplexity.pdf

Wood, P. F. (2008). Reading instruction with gifted and talented readers: A series of unfortunate events or a sequence of auspicious results? *Gifted Child Today, 31*(3), 16–25.

Chapter Five

Key Component: Creative Reading

"To grow intellectually, gifted students need challenging books. They need fiction with complex plots and carefully developed characters, and informational books that explore topics in depth. They should read books and periodicals that spark their imaginations, broaden their horizons, and cause them to wonder and question."—Thomas Gunning (1992)

SCENARIO

Mrs. Saari considers herself a creative thinker and teacher. Her thinking style, categorized as abstract random, sometimes frustrates her colleagues, but her students thrive under it. As a kindergarten teacher, she strives to create a sense of wonder in her newly minted students and is sensitive to those for whom the confines of the traditional eclipses curiosity. Most of her late-5- and early-6-year-old students are just beginning to put together the foundational reading skills of phonemic awareness and inventive spelling—all except one. Jeremy enters her classroom at 5 years and 6 months old. Jeremy is already reading at a fourth-grade level!

Although clearly beyond learning that *A* says *apple* or that we read from left to right and top to bottom, Mrs. Saari notices that Jeremy has a hunger for learning that rivals her own. Jeremy still has to learn how to write his name, his beginning math facts, and what it means to be in a community, like a school, but he does not need to learn how to read. It is time to focus on reading to learn.

Reading to children daily is a nonnegotiable priority for Mrs. Saari. Reading aloud to children stimulates their imaginations and expands their understanding of the world. It helps them develop language and listening skills and prepares them to understand the written word. Mrs. Saari also believes that,

children learn how to read by themselves, it is still important for
to them.

...s year she starts by reading *James and the Giant Peach* by Roald Dahl
(1961). Jeremy has already read this book over the summer before kindergarten. This revelation challenges Mrs. Saari's reading plan until her creative
mind seeks other options. The question becomes, "How can I keep Jeremy
engaged with the class while we read *James and the Giant Peach* and still
move him forward in his own learning?"

It just so happens that year the movie version of *James and the Giant
Peach* comes out. Mrs. Saari finds a way to get Jeremy to respond to the text
from both his own reading of it and a second reading when she reads aloud to
the class. Paired with a parent volunteer, Jeremy's task is to compare the
novel to the movie adaptation and then write up a review of the comparison
to share with the class. Because Jeremy's writing ability does not match his
reading ability, he dictates his insights to a parent volunteer over the course
of the fall semester. He creates a printed version of his analysis that he
illustrates himself and, with the help of Mrs. Saari, binds his own book.
When the class finishes the reading of *James and the Giant Peach*, Jeremy
reads his book to the class and shares his creative response. He remains
motivated throughout, and Mrs. Saari bathes in the satisfaction of her own
creative response to this particular challenge.

Patricia Wood (2008) proposes the following key components of a reading
program for gifted and talented readers:

- Assessment
- Acceleration
- Enrichment
- Opportunities for discussion

Based on the work of gifted-education experts, this book covers many of
these components in an implicit way. The following four chapters propose
more explicit ways to address the remaining key components described by
Wood: creative reading, critical reading, inquiry reading, and flexible grouping.

Creative reading focuses more on gifted readers' responses to text, not the
reading of said text. The text, regardless if it is literary or informational, acts
as the source for a reader's imaginative and original thought production. This
creative thought is produced through writing, performance, invention, or
other divergent response. For example, creative-reading activities for *To Kill
a Mockingbird* (Lee, 1995) might include writing scripts and dramatizations
based on one or more of the scenes in the book, creating an alternative ending

of the trial and a prediction of how that may have affected the community, or creating poetry or artwork that depicts the driving themes in the text.

Creative reading is considered the highest yet most neglected form of reading (Witty, 1985). This is as true now as it was in the 1980s. With a staunch emphasis on standards-based curriculum, teachers allow themselves to feel constrained by the standards and offer very few options for how students can respond to text. Creativity and creative thinking do not appear to be as highly valued as proficiency and mastery. The needs of the gifted reader demand more than proficiency and mastery because often they have already met expectations put forth in the standards.

In order to better prepare opportunities for gifted readers to engage in creative-reading activities, teachers may need to refresh their understanding of creativity and creative thinking prior to designing creative-reading activities.

A BRIEF INTRODUCTION TO CREATIVITY AND CREATIVE THINKING

Creativity is measured on four levels: fluency, flexibility, originality, and elaboration. These levels of creative thought, when considered, can help during ideation (Raudsepp, 1981). When teachers develop ways for gifted readers to respond to text, they are engaged in ideation. Tapping into these levels of creative thought during ideation will produce more divergent responses:

- **Fluency.** The ability to generate and manage a large number of ideas when confronting a task or problem. When we brainstorm ideas without judgment or filtering those ideas, we engage in fluency. The goal is to generate as many ideas as possible.
- **Flexibility.** The companion to fluency in ideation. Flexibility is where we make associations with an initial idea. We ask the questions "What else?" and "What would happen if . . . ?" We consider other categories of information, so we're not locked into one type of idea or solution.
- **Originality.** Although it is widely acknowledged that there are no new ideas, just new ways to look at old ideas, the level of originality in creative thinking makes sure that we pursue more divergent, wilder what-if scenarios during ideation. This is where we look for original ways to solve existing tasks or challenges.
- **Elaboration.** A part of creative thinking and ideation. Elaboration is about increasing the level of detail describing an idea. For example, an idea like "height-adjustable floor" can be expressed as "A height-adjustable floor in a kitchen ensures an ergonomic work position for chefs of various

heights." Elaboration drives shared understanding of ideas and itself can be a source for more ideas. It gives us more to consider during a task or when addressing a challenge or a problem.

In order to adequately plan for creative reading as a key component of reading instruction for gifted readers, educators engage first in their own creative thinking so that they then can model that type of creative thought for their gifted readers. Using these four levels of creative behavior, consider the following creative-reading task:

> In what ways might we explore and communicate our understanding of cultural and ethical perspectives embodied in the novel *To Kill a Mockingbird*?

First, there is power in the question as it is posed. This is a defined task or a problem to solve for gifted students. It is complex, does not have one right answer, and supports creative thinking with depth and complexity. During ideation, educators can plan activities and assignments that address the task or challenge using fluency, flexibility, originality, and elaboration.

Fluency

How many ways can we explore and communicate our understanding of the cultural and ethical perspectives in this book? (A brainstorming list would follow.) Keywords for fluency include:

Compare	List
Convert	Match
Count	Name
Define	Outline
Describe	Paraphrase
Explain	Predict
Identify	Summarize
Label	

Flexibility

Can we categorize those ways we generated during fluency? Can we view the cultural and ethical perspectives through a different lens or a different point of view? Are there other perspectives that might help us look at the cultural and ethical ones in a different light (e.g., societal, personal, historical)? Keywords for flexibility include:

Change	Extrapolate
Demonstrate	Interpolate
Distinguish	Interpret
Employ	Predict

Originality

What if we looked for trials since the time period of *To Kill a Mockingbird* that address similar issues? Can we situate the trial in today's culture and climate? What if we retell the story from another character's point of view instead? What if Tom Robinson were deaf and mute and unable to defend himself? Keywords for originality include:

Compose	Integrate
Create	Rearrange
Design	Reconstruct
Generate	Reorganize
Modify	Revise

Elaboration

Let's add more detail to how we explore and communicate about *To Kill a Mockingbird*. Use a visual metaphor common to the 1950s that is conceptual and not a reflection of realism, and determine the ethical struggle Atticus Finch encounters when defending Tom Robinson. Keywords for elaboration include:

Appraise	Judge
Critique	Measure
Determine	Select
Evaluate	Test
Grade	

STRATEGIES FOR CREATIVE READING

Creative reading invites an imaginative interaction with print (Levande, 1993). The following are suggested strategies for gifted readers as they respond to and interact with text. Some of these strategies work well during the prewriting or writing stages.

Using Imagery

The ability to think in images is one characteristic of creative people. Imagery often contains the seed of a new idea (Raudsepp, 1981). When first understanding an idea or concept, we can imagine it. Language often falls short in communicating our understanding; language can be limiting.

Try to encourage gifted readers to first feel or situate in imagery what they imagine to be a response to text before naming or verbally formulating a response. For example, after reading *To Kill a Mockingbird*, prime the creative-thinking pump by asking students, "Imagine you are Scout, watching her father defend Tom Robinson in the courtroom. What images come to mind that might Scout see with her father?"

Thinking in Metaphors

Metaphor is an effective literary tool, not so much for showing how particular things are alike, but for showing how we can make them alike and how we establish the grounds that allow us to perceive similarity in the first place. Metaphor is a way to create common ground or a shared experience between different parties.

Teachers can use metaphor with gifted readers in two ways: (1) discuss the intentional metaphor in an authored text, and (2) encourage readers to come up with their own metaphors to connect concepts encountered in the text to their lived experiences. For example, in *To Kill a Mockingbird*, the metaphor in the title is often analyzed. A *mockingbird* imitates the calls of other birds; they don't sing their own songs. When we identify with other people, we believe, like mockingbirds, they will sing our songs, conform to our worldviews, abandon their own unique voices, and sing in unison along with us (DiPiero, 2010). When gifted readers respond to text using metaphor, they interact on a deeper, more complex level.

Role-Playing or Simulation

Role-playing can be used to motivate students to learn new material and to reinforce material that already has been learned. It is a great outlet for creative expression or response to text. Role-playing and creative dramatics have been recommended as part of the curriculum for gifted students in the area of language arts (VanTassel-Baska, 1998). In response to the novel *To Kill a Mockingbird*, a simulation of the trial or a reader's theater of parts of the novel offers gifted readers an opportunity to experience the text on a deeper level.

Tolerating Ambiguity

Creative reading requires readers to be open to new ways of thinking and to produce creative ideas or responses to text by not holding onto the familiar or binding habits. This does not mean gifted readers should run to embrace chaos, but instead they should show adaptability, fluidity, and a tolerance for ambiguity (Raudsepp, 1981). One way for gifted readers to demonstrate this strategy is to consider opposing frames or points of view to an either/or or pro/con situation. In *To Kill a Mockingbird*, the issue of whether "good" justice was dealt is considered by readers. Students can respond to this by offering five arguments in favor of good justice and five arguments against good justice. Considering opposite points of view generates creative thinking.

Incorporating Aesthetics Awareness

Arts-based literacy taps into the aesthetic sensitivity or awareness of students. Using images as inspiration, students become more aware of what is pleasing to them and how a particular image makes them feel. Developing an aesthetic awareness allows gifted readers to engage in the literacy task of responding to text in creative ways. Image making (Olshansky, 1995) enables readers to gain fuller power of their expression and response to text. Aesthetics awareness cultivates an attention to detail that may not otherwise be cultivated.

In *To Kill a Mockingbird*, the detailed accounts of the characters and settings offer readers a mindful, arts-based way to respond to the text. Gifted readers reveal the layers of plot and character development in this way.

ALIGNING CREATIVE READING TO STANDARDS

Creative reading is a goal for reading instruction for gifted readers. When gifted readers are grouped together for reading instruction, whether within a traditional classroom or in a gifted classroom, there are planned-for and expected outcomes. The following grade-level content standards, aligned with the NAGC (2010) *Pre-K–Grade 12 Gifted Programming Standards*, can provide gifted readers with opportunities to grow and progress in creative reading:

3.2.1. Educators design curricula in cognitive, affective, aesthetic, social, and leadership domains that are challenging and effective for students with gifts and talents.

3.4.2. Educators use creative-thinking strategies to meet the needs of students with gifts and talents.

ASSESSING CREATIVE READING

Gifted readers may not naturally read creatively; responding to text in a creative way often requires direct instruction. As creative reading is encouraged, it's important to help readers learn what creative reading is and recognize creative responses to text. Then we can assess students' creative-reading abilities.

One way to assess creative-reading behaviors is to use a checklist aligned to the characteristics of creative readers and the research-based creative-reading strategies. The "Creative-Reading Checklist" is used to both identify and monitor creative-reading behaviors (Martin & Cramond, 1984). Rate the creative-reading behaviors on a scale of 1 (seldom) to 5 (often). N/A (not applicable) is used when a student could not be rated because they have not been given the opportunity to demonstrate a given behavior:

1. Expresses feelings or emotions about things read.
2. Applies information read to different settings.
3. Makes guesses about what will happen next.
4. Thinks of other ways the story could have ended.
5. Questions why characters behave certain ways.
6. Adds his or her own ideas to the author's ideas.
7. Compares the author's conclusion with other possible conclusions.
8. Relates what is read to his or her own experience.
9. Visualizes what is read.
10. Expresses how he or she might have changed the story.
11. Sees questions left unanswered by the author.
12. Asks questions that demonstrate insights about things that are read.
13. Gives examples when reading about something.
14. Organizes information obtained while reading to show relationships between things.
15. Discusses what he or she has read as if it has really happened.
16. Uses what is read to solve problems.
17. Uses what is read as a springboard for original ideas.
18. Relates what is read to other things that he or she has read.
19. Questions why the author did certain things.
20. Expresses what he or she would have done in a character's place.

How students are evaluated using such a checklist can directly affect future reading instruction to better develop particular creative-reading behaviors.

* * *

From the Expert

Dr. Dorothy Sisk, endowed chair in education of gifted students, Lamar University

Can you offer teachers some ways to help students use the printed page (text) for imaginative and original thought?

Years ago, as a classroom teacher of eighth-grade students, we discussed the quality of our physical science text, its relevancy to the real world, and the fact that it was outdated. I asked for permission to place the books on the shelf and to write our own text. I think the science supervisor was so shocked that she said, "Yes."

We had a special ceremony as each student solemnly placed their physical science texts on the shelf. Then we took the chapter titles and broke into small groups to list the major topics to be covered and activities that were meaningful. We had 10 chapters and 30 students. We listed the topics on the board: "Properties of Matter," "The Structure of Matter," "Motion," "Work and Heat," "Energy and Changes in Matter," "Sound," "Light," "Electric Charges and Currents," "Electrochemical Energy," and "Nuclear Energy." The students placed their names beside the chapter that they wanted to work on, and the groups of three evolved.

As they researched and talked with one another, their creativity kicked in with what they called extending activities, which they carried out to make sure they worked. One father who taught at a nearby college was intrigued with our project and volunteered to print it for us in a binder that could be distributed to other science teachers. It was amusing to see students go back to their old texts to ensure that they were adapting the material to current times. They often used the printed page of the old text and used more engaging language, and I have to say, listening to them was amazing, as their critical thinking kicked in to stimulate a more unique way to present an idea or concept.

How might teachers make room for creative reading as a program component that includes the needs of culturally and linguistically diverse students?

In today's classrooms, most of the students are going to be culturally or linguistically diverse. For example, in Texas 52% of the students are Hispanic, and in my hometown of Port Arthur, at least 10% of the students are Vietnamese. As I visited one class last week, the teacher said she had 12 different languages in her class. She had her class involved in critical thinking in reading using their first language to extend thinking, providing scaffolding and maintaining high expectations. Many of the strategies she used were similar to the SWIRL (speaking and writing integrated with reading and listening) strategy.

One of my colleagues, Elsa Anderson (2015), wrote a chapter in our book *Engaging and Effective Strategies for English Language Learners*, and she visited my university (Lamar) and worked with our middle school students who were culturally and linguistically diverse. Two of her strategies that were well received included "Words in, Words Out" and "Question Ladders."

Strategy: Words in, Words Out
Cultural and linguistic scaffolding:

- Ask students about their favorite book.
- Discuss text orientation based on the language in which the book is written.
- Model a think-aloud with a different book, and demonstrate words in and out.
- Encourage use of first language as needed for discussion or self-talk.

Materials:

- Text to be read
- List of words: Include some words taken from the text to be read and others that do not appear in the text.

Procedures:

1. Read the title of the text before starting. When applicable (if reading from a book), show the cover to the students.
2. Ask students: After hearing the title of the text that you will read and using your prior knowledge of the topic, think about:

   Which words from the list do you think will appear in the text? Why?

   Which words from the list do you think will be excluded from the text? Why?

3. Students work in pairs or small groups to evaluate each word in the context of the topic and title. After discussion, each group presents a justification of why they grouped each word as an "in" or an "out" word. Students read the text (or the teacher can read it aloud while students listen for the specific words).
4. After reading, students evaluate their lists and adjust as needed. Each group prepares an explanation about why changes were made to their original word predictions.

Rationale:

This strategy allows students to activate prior knowledge on a topic. Students build vocabulary through discussion and reading and use higher-order thinking through analysis and justification of reasoning.

Strategy: Question Ladders
Cultural and linguistic scaffolding:

- Provide vocabulary support to accomplish the task by discussing words that can be used.
- Model the strategy one component at a time.
- Monitor and continue to provide oral and written language as needed.
- Encourage use of first language as needed for discussion or self-talk.

Materials:

- Reading materials on a topic or unit of study
- Colored paper
- Writing utensils

Procedures:

1. Make a two-flap book. On the left flap, write a list of the three most important facts about this topic. Leave some space between each fact. Students may use resources to select important facts (depending on the teacher's objectives for this strategy). On the right flap, develop questions using the following sentence stems for each question:

   What ... ?
   Why ... ?
   What if ... ?

2. Pair up with someone, and trade flap books, answering each other's questions. Select one of the questions and answers, and develop it into a draft to be shared with the class.

Rationale:
This strategy provides students an opportunity to demonstrate knowledge and comprehension of a topic and, at the same time, to determine importance. Students can then think critically when creating higher-level questions related to that topic. ELLs are provided with many opportunities to develop and expand academic language.

What barriers to creative reading do you think teachers encounter, and what advice do you have for them to overcome these barriers?

Sadly, most states have statewide testing, and teachers are fearful to venture beyond state standards, and much classroom time is dedicated to preparing for the statewide tests with worksheet after worksheet. One way to secure freedom from this regimen would be for teachers to write proposals for grants to develop and implement creative experiences in reading.

In addition, teachers could dedicate five minutes in the beginning of class with a short read-aloud to the students and then post sets of discussion questions. The students can select a partner and interact in discussions with one another. The number of student-student interactions could be tallied for each student, and rewards could be given to the students with the most points each week.

The rewards can be generated from the students: What would you like to have as a winner of the discussion sets? Some of the rewards students have listed include lunch with the teacher, extra time on the computer (15 minutes), work with younger students in their class (reading to them), selecting books from the library for the class, visiting with the principal as a helper, and so on. What is amazing is that their idea of rewards seems to include doing something constructive and being active. That should be a clue to us as educators that students don't want to be passive.

One of my favorite creative-reading strategies was suggested by Margaret Bynum, a former state consultant for the gifted in Georgia. The teacher selects a book and then decorates a box to depict one of the characters in the book. Then, the teacher creates activities to be placed in envelopes that the students can take out and work on alone or with a partner. The activities again could be developed around a model, perhaps Bloom or, my favorite, Calvin Taylor's "Creative Totem Poles" (academic, prediction, creative, communication, decision making, and implementation). These are not graded; they are just fun ways to involve students in creative reading. Some of the barriers may be in the heads of teachers; they may think that doing creative reading won't ensure good scores on tests. In fact, in some cases where teachers asked to be free from "getting ready for the state tests" and provided creative projects, those students had significantly higher scores on statewide tests.

* * *

ASSIGNMENT: THINK-TAC-TOE MATRIX FOR
CREATIVE READING RESPONSES

Using an extension menu to promote creative-reading responses to text provides for the depth and complexity needs of gifted readers. Create a Think-Tac-Toe extension menu as a way to effectively differentiate for a single

gifted reader or a group of gifted readers. Allow students to chooᵣ
menu, and then evaluate their process, product, or performance in lig...
common core and NAGC (2010) standards. Consider the extension menu foɪ
To Kill a Mockingbird in Table 5.1.

Table 5.1. Think-Tac-Toe for *To Kill a Mockingbird*

Create a drawing of some aspect or scene of the novel that comes to life for you. Be sure your drawing depicts the person, place, or thing as Scout describes it. Beneath your picture include a quotation from the novel that refers to your picture and the page number where the description can be found.	Write a bio-poem for any of the major characters in *Mockingbird*, such as Scout, Atticus, Jem, Tom Robinson, Boo, or Mayella. The directions are included on the back of the paper.	One of the most important themes (and lessons in life) is that appearances are deceiving—things are not always what they seem, especially if you have not walked in the shoes of another. Write about an experience in which you misjudged something or someone. What did you learn through this experience?
On a sheet of poster board, make a collage that represents a theme, character, or event in the story. The collage should have a paragraph attached, explaining the theme, character, or event that you have visually presented in your collage.	Find a song or poem that shares a common theme with *Mockingbird*. Type the lyrics to this song or poem. After this, give a two-paragraph explanation that relates the song's meaning to the theme in *Mockingbird*. Use specific examples from the text and specific references to the lyrics or poem.	Make a double bubble to compare and contrast the events, setting, and characteristics of the Scottsboro trials to the settings, events, and characteristics of the trial of Tom Robinson.
Write a SPINE poem. Select a meaningful line from anywhere in the novel. There are hundreds of potential lines that stand out as meaningful, profound, worth repeating, and worth thinking about throughout the novel. The words must occur in the same order as they appear in the quote but should not appear consecutively. The words form the backbone of the poem. The theme of the poem should relate in some way to the line itself or the novel or both.	Create a mock Facebook page for Scout, Jem, Dill, or Boo Radley. The template for this project can be found on Ms. Hayes's English I website. Just look under "Documents."	Imagine you are a member of the jury who has heard the case of Tom Robinson. Write a letter to your fellow members to convince them of Tom's innocence. Use examples from the text to support your opinion.

REFLECT

Do you engage in creative-reading behaviors? It may be difficult to cultivate these behaviors in your students if you do not possess them yourself.

REFERENCES

Dahl, R. (1961). *James and the giant peach, a children's story*. New York: Knopf.

DiPiero, T. (2010, September–October). Two ways of looking at a mockingbird. *Rochester Review, 73*(1), 16–17.

Gunning, T. (1992). *Creating reading instruction for all children*. Boston: Allyn & Bacon.

Lee, H. (1995). *To kill a mockingbird* (35th anniversary ed.). New York: HarperCollins.

Levande, D. (1993). Identifying and serving the gifted reader. *Reading Improvement, 30*(3), 147–50.

Martin, C. E., & Cramond, B. (1984). A checklist for assessing and developing creative reading. *Gifted Child Today, 7*(2), 22–24. Retrieved from https://doi.org/10.1177%2F107621758400700211

National Association for Gifted Children (NAGC). (2010, November). *NAGC Pre-K–Grade 12 Gifted Programming Standards: A Blueprint for Quality Gifted Education Programs*. Washington, DC: Author. Retrieved from http://www.nagc.org/sites/default/files/standards/K-12%20standards%20booklet.pdf

Olshansky, B. (1995). Picture this: An arts-based literacy program. *Educational Leadership, 53*(1), 44–47. Retrieved from http://www.ascd.org/publications/educational_leadership/sept95/vol53/num01/Picture_This@_An_Arts-Based_Literacy_Program.aspx

Raudsepp, E. (1981). *How creative are you? A fun program for measuring and expanding your creative potential*. New York: G. P. Putnam's Sons.

VanTassel-Baska, J. (1998). *Excellence in educating gifted and talented learners* (3rd ed.). Denver, CO: Love.

Witty, P. A. (1985). Rationale for fostering creative reading in the gifted and the creative. In M. Labuda (ed.), *Creative reading for gifted learners* (2nd ed., pp. 8–25). Newark, DE: International Reading Association.

Wood, P. F. (2008). Reading instruction with gifted and talented readers: A series of unfortunate events or a sequence of auspicious results? *Gifted Child Today, 31*(3), 16–24.

Chapter Six

Key Component: Critical Reading

"Knowing a great deal is not the same as being smart; intelligence is not information alone but also judgment, the manner in which information is collected and used."—Carl Sagan

SCENARIO

The students in Ms. Hoffman's fifth-grade class, in an International Baccalaureate school, are in the process of studying the theme "Who We Are," which focuses on different perspectives and viewpoints, when they began a unit called "News and Noteworthy." The unit is designed to expose students to the ways that different points of view and biases can affect the information they receive.

Ms. Hoffman begins by selecting newspaper clippings of current events and charges her students with reading the articles and discerning the importance of both the topic and the medium. Students have an opportunity to discuss the purpose of newspapers, as well as to begin thinking about the role of perspective in both reporting and reading about events.

Once her students achieve some background into the news media and some familiarity with reading this type of content, Ms. Hoffman introduces the concept of bias by connecting it to the current political climate's rallying cry of "fake news." Students watch a video and read an article about the components of verifiable news. They then have the task of locating a news story on the internet and determining its veracity using a checklist. The checklist includes deciding whether the website is a reliable news organization, finding a byline (if there is one), and being cautious about the changing nature of "breaking news."

The students are engaged throughout the activity and find many examples of breaking news to report to their classmates. Through their discussions, the students demonstrate an understanding of how to use critical-thinking skills to discriminate between what is real and what is not, as well as a sense of pride in their own abilities to be educated consumers of news.

One of the final lessons in the unit is for the students to take on a specific perspective through a debate. Ms. Hoffman leads the class through a brainstorming activity of current events topics. Students have a number of ideas, including "Should teachers carry guns in school?" and "Should there be an age restriction for senior citizens who drive?" but they settle on "Should students be allowed to have cell phones in schools?" After being selected randomly for a specific side, students research and present their findings. While it is difficult at first for them to consider arguments from a viewpoint different from their own, they later acknowledge that thinking about the other perspective has broadened their understanding of the issue.

Once gifted readers move beyond the goal of foundational reading skills, instruction should move forward from skill development to inferential and interpretive reading instruction. Critical reading goes well beyond the five pillars of literacy and requires readers to evaluate text and decide its applicability, practicality, and relevance.

Critical reading is process oriented, not product oriented. The use of critical thinking and critical language prepares readers for deeper understandings and application through challenging literature. The teacher's job is to prepare readers with the skills to read this challenging literature. Wood (2008) describes the following critical-reading skills to include in a program for gifted readers:

- Analyze text to detect author bias.
- Infer hidden meanings.
- Locate, organize, and synthesize information related to a given topic.
- Understand elements in literature, including figures of speech, connotations, idioms, plot, characterizations, setting, and voice.

High intellectual ability does not guarantee critical thinking or critical reading. Critical reading is an advanced reading goal that must be included in the curriculum for gifted readers in an intentional way. Critical reading includes the attributes of critical thinking and critical language. Attention to building skill sets within each propels gifted readers forward into responding to text in a deep and complex way.

CRITICAL THINKING AND CRITICAL READERS

Critical thinking has been a traditional focus of gifted programs. As such, it has its critics. In a study conducted by the National Center for Research on Gifted Education (Long et al., 2019), 2,000 schools were surveyed. The study found that teachers of gifted students focus primarily on activities that develop critical thinking and creativity, but the focus on providing advanced reading and writing instruction fell to 19th on their list of priorities. Gifted students showed slower academic growth than their typical peers.

Critical thinking is an important skill if it is paired with the goal of accessing and responding to advanced and challenging material. In isolation, critical thinking is a tool without a problem to solve. The following methods can be taught to meet the goal of critical reading of advanced and challenging material.

Argumentation

Argumentation is the ability to analyze a problem, present an assertion, provide data to support your assertion, and then provide a grounded conclusion. A conclusion without data or evidence is not argumentation; it is opinion (Tirri & Pehkonen, 2002). The process as outlined allows gifted readers to deal expertly with abstract theories or problems and provides them with a way to respond that is grounded in facts.

The critical-thinking skill of argumentation can be used when gifted readers engage with accelerated or advanced texts. This skill is not relegated to the Advanced Placement English class but can be incorporated in any ELA (English language arts) curriculum at any level. Argumentation begins with a question that situates a problem or theory in the abstract or hypothetical for readers.

Consider the book *The Giver* (Lowry, 1993), in which Jonas, the main character, lives in a world that is perfect. Everything is under control. There is no war or fear or pain. There are no choices. Every person is assigned a role in the community. Start with a question that taps the abstract, hypothetical, or existential problem or theme, and facilitate readers' argumentation responses:

- Should the collective good outweigh the rights of an individual?
- Is the pursuit of perfection a reasonable quest?

Following the argumentation process, gifted readers respond to the text, in this case, *The Giver*, through the vehicle of the abstract, hypothetical, or existential questions.

The Scientific Method

As critical readers engage in interpretive and inferential activities, they can use a structured process for uncovering truth about the underlying themes of an advanced or challenging text. The scientific method is not relegated to the sciences; it can also be applied to problems in literary or informational texts. Learning the steps in the scientific method and then applying those steps in a different context, like during character analysis in a novel, gives the reader a structured way to address the main problem (Caruana, 2004). The scientific method helps the reader minimize bias or prejudice during problem solving. The steps in the scientific method that can be applied during critical reading are:

- State the question or problem.
- Form a hypothesis to explain it.
- Test the hypothesis through experimentation.
- Draw conclusions.

Applied to an advanced literary text like *The Giver*, readers can address the main character's problem or main conflict. Jonas is assigned in the Community to be the Receiver of Memories. The main conflict for Jonas is that he now knows all the memories of the Community that no one else knows or can know. This causes him to question the society he lives in and the restrictions set upon the Community by the Elders.

The problem Jonas faces is the way the Community runs. The Elders set many restrictions on the Community, and no one knows a different way to live. But because Jonas is receiving such vivid images, he wants the rest of the Community to feel as he feels. However, as a Receiver of Memories, he is not permitted to share what he sees.

State the question or problem. Now that Jonas knows the truth of his Community, he wants everyone to know the truth and have free will. The Community will not allow this. Jonas wants harmony.

Form a hypothesis to explain it. Jonas is experiencing cognitive dissonance: What he believes and what he is experiencing are at odds. In order to gain harmony, Jonas must either change what he believes to match what he is experiencing, or he must change what he is experiencing to match what he believes.

Test the hypothesis through experimentation. Jonas first tries to change what he believes to match what he is experiencing. He takes pride in his position as Receiver of Memories and works hard to learn all he can about his responsibilities so that he contributes to the common good of the Community. This does not work. He becomes more conflicted and begins to tell those he cares about the truth of their Community. He is still experiencing disharmony and desperately needs to reconcile this. Jonas ultimately takes another approach. He changes what he is experiencing to match what he believes. Jonas leaves the Community.

Draw conclusions. Jonas wants harmony and free will. He cannot have either within the Community now that he is the Receiver of Memories. The only way for Jonas to resolve this conflict is to leave the Community.

Deductive Reasoning

Drawing conclusions based on what is already known is called deductive reasoning. Logic applies the skill of deductive reasoning to look for patterns and sets of relationships (Caruana, 2004). Logic allows the gifted reader to ask the question, "Does that conclusion follow the facts as I know them?" The critical-thinking skills of logic and deductive reasoning offer gifted readers a path to navigate the murky waters of moral dilemmas, unsettled law, myths, and complex literary themes that present themselves in texts in and out of school.

Logic includes knowing how to apply fallacies (errors in logical thinking), establishing a premise, presenting an argument, and stating a conclusion. Presenting an argument and stating a conclusion are both covered earlier in this chapter. In order to facilitate logical thinking and apply that logic as part of a critical-reading goal, gifted readers benefit from some formal logic training.

In their book *The Well-Trained Mind*, Jessie Wise and Susan Wise Bauer (1999, p. 242) use the story of Snow White to illustrate the five fallacies. Any one of these fallacies could have caused Snow White to allow the wicked witch—disguised as a peasant woman pedaling apples—to trick her into eating a poisoned piece of fruit:

1. **Anecdotal evidence fallacy.** Using a personal experience to prove a point: *I've met peasant women before, and none of them ever poisoned me, Snow White thinks to herself.*
2. **Argumentum ad hominem.** An attack on the speaker rather than on the argument itself. The peasant woman attacks the dwarves' motives: *"Did the dwarves tell you not to let anyone in? They just want you to keep on cooking their meals and scrubbing their floors."*
3. **Argumentum ad misericordiam.** An appeal to pity: *"I'm just a poor peasant woman trying to earn a penny for my sick children. You should let me in."*
4. **Argumentum ad verecundiam.** An appeal to authority. It may use the name of a famous person in support of an assertion: *"I just sold an apple to the king, and he said it was the best apple he ever ate!"*

5. **Argumentum ad lazarum.** The assumption that a poor person is automatically more virtuous than a rich person: *"I'm just a simple beggar woman, so I'd never hurt you."*

If you take a close look at these fallacies, you notice them everywhere. Political speeches, publicity campaigns, election slogans, newspaper editorials, and even textbooks use faulty logic to sway readers to a different point of view.

Logical thinking has three stages. The first is the premise; there may be more than one premise. The key is to help gifted readers make sure that the first premise is true before drawing any conclusions based on it. The argument will determine the validity of the premise. A false premise will always yield a false conclusion:

Premise A: The earth is a flat surface.
Premise B: It is possible to fall off the edge of a flat surface.
Conclusion: It is possible to fall off the edge of the earth.

Premise A: The magic mirror always tells the truth.
Premise B: The mirror says that Snow White is more beautiful than I.
Conclusion: Snow White is more beautiful than I.

This conclusion is valid, based on the premise of the story.

Simplify this logical reasoning by replacing these premises with *if/then* statements. If *the magic mirror always tells the truth,* and *the mirror says Snow White is more beautiful than I am,* then *Snow White is more beautiful than I am.*

If the first statement is true and the logic is not faulty, then the conclusion will always be true. As we teach gifted readers how to respond to text (no matter its form) using logic as a part of critical thinking, we help them discover for themselves the truth and the right conclusions.

CRITICAL LANGUAGE AND CRITICAL READERS

Critical language skills include those elements in literature that allow readers to access deeper meaning. Figures of speech, idioms, connotations, and vocabulary building through morphological study all contribute to the gifted reader's ability to respond to challenging and advanced texts. Critical language study emphasizes the development of analysis and interpretation skills. It also includes formal study of English grammar and vocabulary. VanTassel-Baska (2003) proposes that critical language study should promote vocabulary development in order to foster an "understanding of word relationships (analogies) and origins (etymology), and [to develop] an appreciation for semantics, linguistics, and the history of language" (p. 4). In this way, critical language helps readers to learn deeply, question choices, deal with dilemmas, and synthesize prior and present learning when encountering advanced texts.

A FOCUS ON WORD ORIGINS (ETYMOLOGY)

Latin and Greek linguistic patterns offer gifted readers a way to leverage academic vocabulary to support a deeper understanding of complex and advanced texts. Teaching Latin and Greek roots, prefixes, and suffixes helps readers generalize their learning in such a way that they are able to comprehend and discern deeper meaning of texts they encounter. Latin and Greek roots can be taught in the primary, intermediate, and middle grades and are not relegated to only the secondary grades (Rasinski, Padak, Newton, & Newton, 2011). Although there is not an agreed-upon list of appropriate word roots worth teaching at different grade levels, teaching them moves readers from the familiar to the unfamiliar.

For example, help gifted readers sort words by their roots to gain a deeper and more nuanced understanding. Following the root-sorting process of Templeton and Gehsmann (2014), focus on two Latin roots with opposite meanings: - *bell-* ("war") and - *pax-* or -*pac-* ("peace"). Show the following words: *rebellion, pacify, belligerent, pacifist, antebellum, pact, bellicose, pacific.*

Have students sort the words by their roots. Then engage in a discussion of meanings. Some of these words have prefixes that hold their own meanings. Ensure readers understand those meanings before discussing the meanings of the full words. For example, discuss that *rebellion* has to do with returning or waging war on someone in authority. Model and explain how to uncover the meanings of words using the roots and affixes. Encourage readers to then think through how -*bell-* and - *pax-* or -*pac-* combine with prefixes and suffixes to create other words. As readers learn how to think critically about the different units of meaning in words, their sense of inquiry will be heightened, and their ability to deal with more abstract texts increases exponentially.

MORAL REASONING AS AN ACCESS POINT FOR CRITICAL READING

Reflecting on moral dilemmas and providing argumentation for their moral reasoning is an important attribute to critical reading for gifted readers. Although high intellectual ability does not necessarily predict high moral judgment (Tirri & Pehkonen, 2002), as gifted readers engage in advanced texts and sometimes more mature texts, they encounter moral dilemmas. These encounters require a response. Teachers who work with gifted readers should nurture their moral reasoning abilities by reflecting on moral dilemmas found in different areas of study. Being able to effectively argue through a moral dilemma helps to build an ethical conscience.

For example, during a study of native peoples during a Florida history unit in fourth grade, a class does an investigation of the ceremonial shell mounds of the Tocobaga Indians. After studying the Spanish colonization of Florida, which destroyed many of the native tribes and their cultures, students encounter a moral dilemma. While clearing the land meant for a new subdivision, contractors discovered evidence of a long-lost shell mound. Construction on the site was halted, and an archeological dig proceeded to determine the legitimacy of the shell mound. *Which should be preserved? The ancient shell mound and the culture of the Tocobaga or the high-value real estate deal that would add millions to the county's tax base? Who has the greater claim?* In order to answer these questions, gifted readers must access and respond to a variety of texts and media, with a focus on finding evidence to support their moral reasoning.

Is there any value to preserving or remembering the past? Is the value of the past more important than the value of present endeavors? Students will have to consider an even bigger question, one that every generation has faced: *Does the end justify the means?* This basic ethical argument, rooted in Machiavellian perspective, crosses every area of study. Critical reading offers students the tools they need to consider this and other moral dilemmas.

* * *

From the Expert
Dr. Frances Spielhagen, professor of education and cofounder and codirector of the Center for Adolescent Research and Development, Mount Saint Mary College

No one disputes the importance of critical-reading skills and activities for gifted, accelerated, or "early mastery" learners. However, at this point, I strongly encourage you not to get hung up on the concept of giftedness and how we identify those students. That pursuit has bedeviled our profession for more than 40 years. My focus is those students in your classes who are clearly functioning beyond the other students, those who need and deserve the opportunity to delve more deeply, reading texts that are appropriate for their interests and abilities. You know who they are!

Our priority must be selecting appropriate texts for students to explore using critical-reading skills and strategies. Vygotsky reminds us, "If the environment presents no such [challenging] tasks to the student . . . and does not stimulate his intellect by providing a sequence of new goals, his thinking fails to reach the highest stages, or reaches them with great delay."

E. M. Forster, the English novelist further reminds us, "The only books that influence us are those for which we are ready, and which have gone a little further down our particular path than we have gone ourselves." Too often, advanced readers spend their precious time and talent reading texts below their ability levels or waiting for others to catch up with them.

Sally Reis cites a quote in *To Kill a Mockingbird* that captures Scout's feeling of frustration when she is required to not go beyond the text read by the rest of the class: "I mumbled that I was sorry and retired meditating upon my crime." In that moment Scout realizes that she loves reading and hates school! Many years have passed since Scout was in school, and hopefully, in the face of standardized learning modules, teachers like you are striving to move beyond that dire situation.

Assuming that you and your students have selected an appropriate text at the appropriate level of difficulty, the next task is to foster the critical-thinking skills that allow students to explore that text fully. In this regard, I encourage you to refer to your knowledge of Bloom's Taxonomy.

Too often, we feel compelled to start at the bottom and work up the Bloom ladder. Gifted readers must move beyond the basic knowledge and comprehension, at the very least to application and analysis of the text. Think of it this way: Who, what, where, and when questions are not as important as the *why* (application and analysis) and *what if* (evaluation and synthesis) questions. By the way, Bloom himself was alleged to have said that in no way did he advise people to start at the bottom of the taxonomy and work up but that, instead, knowledge is the core of all the levels and one can enter at any point.

The current emphasis on using nonfiction texts allows ample opportunity for implementation of higher-order questioning. However, for young readers, early fictional chapter books like the Magic Tree House series by Mary Pope Osborne set the stage for critical-thinking explorations of the context for those stories, like ancient Egypt, the rainforest, and Mount Vesuvius. The series also contains companion nonfiction books for some of the titles, allowing the gifted reader to pursue a topic in greater depth, while classmates may be reading the fictional adventures of the two protagonists.

In a similar way, students in the middle grades can read fictional books like *My Brother Sam Is Dead* (Collier & Collier, 1974) and then explore the events of the American Revolution that actually took place and set the context for that book, as well as author bias and point of view. Moreover, the range of texts available for students particularly at this level must include multicultural voices on the human experience (e.g., war and revolution).

In this age of "fake news," high school students must practice sifting and sorting through the explosion of information they encounter on social media and in the written texts they read. The Stanford History Education Group (SHEG) provides a vast array of teacher resources for fostering critical reading in adolescent students, with some also appropriate for younger students.

Joyce VanTassel-Baska, who literally wrote the book on curriculum for high-ability learners, recommends that such learners develop analytical and interpretative skills by citing similarities and differences among texts on the same topic and also among selected pieces of literature. They should define the problems presented in the texts they read and explore possible solutions. Ultimately, critical reading must also include metacognition, where students reflect on what they are thinking and how and *if* their arguments hold together and make sense, as seen in teacher questions like "What is your evidence for that?" "How do you know that is valid?" and "What is your plan for exploring this topic further? What do you want to learn about next?"

For the gifted learner, the final lesson must be that there is always more to see, encounter, and explore. If school comes easily to them, then they must begin to understand and embrace the challenge that there is more for them to learn beyond the situation they are in. They may be the smartest student in that class, but they also must be ready for challenges beyond their own experiences.

* * *

CRITICAL READING AND ALIGNING TO STANDARDS

Critical reading is the second goal for reading instruction for gifted readers. When gifted readers are grouped together for reading instruction, whether in a traditional classroom or in a gifted classroom, there are planned-for and expected outcomes. The following grade-level content standards, aligned with the NAGC (2010) *Pre-K–Grade 12 Gifted Programming Standards*, provide gifted readers with opportunities to grow and make progress in critical reading:

   3.1.3. Educators adapt, modify, or replace the core or standard curriculum to meet the needs of students with gifts and talents and those with special needs such as twice-exceptional, highly gifted, and English language learners.
   3.4.1. Educators use critical-thinking strategies to meet the needs of students with gifts and talents.

CONCLUSION

Critical reading, as a goal for advanced reading instruction for gifted and accelerated readers, combines the attributes of critical thinking and critical language in order to prepare readers for critical analysis of advanced and oftentimes abstract texts. The key is to ensure that both attributes are taught in tandem with advanced and accelerated content and not in isolation. Teachers must first think critically about content and how to access it before they can facilitate those very same habits of mind in their students.

ASSIGNMENT

Reading strategy instruction should include critical-thinking questions about deep meaning in text that are

- literal,
- inferential,
- analytical,
- metacognitive, and
- intertextual.

Select a text that is appropriate for advanced readers in your class.

Create a series of Bloom-aligned questions related to that reading, using the following resources:

"Task-Oriented Question Construction Wheel," http://ateneu.xtec.cat/wikiform/wikiexport/_media/cmd/lle/clsa/modul_2/blooms_taxonomy_polygon.pdf

"Bloom's Taxonomy Wheel/Circle-Wall/Poster Display," http://www.in2edu.com/resources/thinking_resources/blooms_taxonomy_chart.pdf

Write the questions on color-coded paper according to the level of difficulty. Place the questions in a large jar or fishbowl. Encourage students to choose questions that are higher order. This can be done in teams or as individuals. Award points for the questions, starting with 1 point for knowledge level and up to 6 points.

REFLECT

There's a chance you may have to defend alternative literacy strategies you choose to employ with your gifted readers. Engage in some critical thinking yourself, and consider both sides of the argument for and against using alternative reading strategies with gifted readers. Make sure you can articulate the evidence to support your stance in your rationale.

REFERENCES

Bloom, B. S. (1969). *Taxonomy of educational objectives: The classification of educational goals : Handbook I, Cognitive domain.* New York: McKay.

Caruana, V. (2004). *Giving your child the excellence edge: 10 traits your child needs to achieve lifelong success.* Grand Rapids, MI: Zondervan.

Collier, J. L., & Collier, C. (1974). *My brother Sam is dead.* New York: Four Winds Press.

Long, D., Hamilton, R., Mccoach, B., Siegle, D., Gubbins, E. J., & Callahan, C. M. (2019, April 9). *National Center for Research on Gifted Education (NCRGE) brief on gifted education curriculum and gifted achievement growth of gifted students in three states.* Storrs: University of Connecticut.

Lowry, L. (1993). *The giver.* Boston: Houghton Mifflin.

National Association for Gifted Children (NAGC). (2010, November). *NAGC Pre-K–Grade 12 Gifted Programming Standards: A Blueprint for Quality Gifted Education Programs.* Washington, DC: Author. Retrieved from http://www.nagc.org/sites/default/files/standards/K-12%20standards%20booklet.pdf

Rasinski, T. V., Padak, N., Newton, J., & Newton, E. (2011). The Latin-Greek connection: Building vocabulary through morphological study. *Reading Teacher, 65*(2), 133–141.

Templeton, S., & Gehsmann, K. (2014). *Teaching reading and writing: The developmental approach (PreK–8).* Boston: Pearson.

Tirri, K., & Pehkonen, L. (2002). The moral reasoning and scientific argumentation of gifted adolescents. *Journal of Secondary Gifted Education, 13*(3), 120–129.

VanTassel-Baska, J. (2003). Differentiating the language arts for high ability learners. *ERIC Clearinghouse on Disabilities and Gifted Education,* ED4744306.

Vygotsky, L. S. (1978). *Mind in society: The development of higher psychological processes.* Cambridge, MA: Harvard University Press.

Wise, J., & Bauer, S. W. (1999). *The well-trained mind.* New York: W. W. Norton.

Wood, P. F. (2008). Reading instruction with gifted and talented readers: A series of unfortunate events or a sequence of auspicious results? *Gifted Child Today, 31*(3), 16–25.

Chapter Seven

Key Component: Inquiry Reading

"True wisdom comes to each of us when we realize how little we understand about life, ourselves, and the world around us."—Socrates

SCENARIO

On April 20, 2010, the scope and sequence of Ms. Green's sixth-grade earth science class in the Tampa Bay area of Florida shifts its trajectory from astronomy to water ecosystems. A wellhead on the Deepwater Horizon oil rig had recently exploded, and it would spew 4.9 million barrels of oil over the next 4 months into the Gulf of Mexico. Ms. Green keeps the television on in her classroom all that day so that each of her successive gifted science classes could have a chance to react to the devastating news.

Using this disaster as a teachable moment, she starts a "parking lot" for questions on chart paper. She encourages students to write their questions and concerns on sticky notes and post them throughout the day. By the end of day 1 (out of 4 months, 4 weeks, and 2 days) of this disaster, students' questions and concerns include the following:

- What caused the spill?
- How do we stop the oil from spreading?
- Will the oil reach our beaches?
- How can we clean this up? Who will clean it up?
- Does this spill affect our water quality?
- What will happen to the marine life in the Gulf?
- Whose fault is this?

And . . .

• Should drilling be allowed so close to our coast?

Questioning is the beginning of wisdom—and the scientific inquiry process. Asking meaningful questions and then working toward finding the answers is the central tenet of inquiry learning. Reading for information in order to answer the questions is therefore the central purpose for reading in inquiry learning. Gifted and accelerated readers with higher comprehension levels need a reading focus on evaluation, synthesis, and analysis; inquiry reading puts the focus on these skills.

The process Ms. Green's students use to answer the meaningful questions they pose about the BP spill takes them 6 weeks to address. Some questions cannot be answered completely. Others give birth to more questions. Still others move them to action and activism.

WHAT IS INQUIRY-BASED LEARNING AND INQUIRY READING?

As a pedagogical approach, inquiry-based learning is student centered and focuses on the quest to answer questions students pose by experimenting and evaluating a variety of solutions. Teachers and students co-construct meaningful learning experiences. The teacher is the facilitator. Students are the explorers.

Most often the process begins with teachers posing open-ended questions they themselves do not know the answers to or those with multiple possible answers. This first question is tied to the teacher's learning objectives and essential learning of the content area. Then, the teacher follows the students' lead by listening to their thoughts about the posed question and then providing or pointing students toward the resources they need to answer their own questions. This process should be made visible throughout and shared with others when the inquiry is complete. In this way we document the learning process and honor the deep dive our students take to bring to the surface valued and valuable solutions.

After a month of caring for a dozen bins full of red wiggler worms in order to find out which foods help produce the most worms and worm casings, Ms. Nocella walks into her classroom one unseasonably cold morning only to find dozens of worms dead on the ground. The worms had escaped their plastic bins and fell from the lab tables onto the cold and colorless linoleum floor.

Within minutes her sixth-grade gifted students enter the room, not knowing the carnage that awaits them. Ms. Guercia stops them from trampling their science experiment and asks, "Why did the worms leave their bins?"

Stunned and confused at the deaths of what they had begun to think of as their class pets, students begin to focus on the problem at hand. "How many did we lose?" asks Terry.

"Did they all escape from one bin?" Eva queries.

"This is just like when I see worms on the sidewalk after it rains," Tiffany muses.

"Was something wrong with their bin?" Rebecca wonders.

"When did this happen?" Mikay asks.

"Could this happen again?" Alyssa worries.

"All good questions," Ms. Guercia says. "I guess we need to get to the bottom of this so we can make sure it never happens again."

"Well, that will only be true if the answer is something we can control," Terry reminds them.

Moments later the students create work groups to answer their burning questions. One group inspects each of the 20 bins to determine how many were lost and from which bins. Another group researches the circumstances when worms might leave their homes. Another group looks for prior research that might indicate a reason for this behavior. Finally, the last group reviews all of the conditions of their red wiggler worm experiment to see if any had changed. The inquiry that ensues takes several days to complete. Information is gathered; conclusions are reached; a summary is shared; and recommended solutions are posed.

Whether part of the inquiry-based learning process or as an independent reading-program goal, inquiry reading is a strategy in which readers take the opportunity to conduct their own independent research in an area of interest to them (Wood, 2008). Students read to answer previously posed questions and further their investigations. Reading for information is the express purpose for this reading strategy. This strategy, when combined with background knowledge, enables our students to construct new knowledge. The following is a collection of skills and steps for students to practice honing their inquiry learning:

1. **Posing Questions.** The questions posed lead the way into the inquiry. Then students follow their lead.

   "Who is ultimately responsible for this off-shore drilling disaster?"

2. **Making Predictions.** Based on the questions posed, students can then make predictions about possible answers to those questions. These predictions propel them through various texts in order to determine whether their predictions are correct.

   "If off-shore drilling is not permitted so close to our shores, then I think we could prevent a disaster like this in the future."

3. **Drawing Inferences.** Based on their predictions, students can then wrestle with what they read and decide for themselves the deeper meaning of the texts.

   "It seems like we should focus on how to prevent this type of disaster in the future because we can't change what happened in the past. What steps can we take as a society to prevent this from ever happening again?"

4. **Determining Main Ideas.** Students then sift through the information they've gained through their reading and determine their relative importance. At this point in the investigation, students should cite their information in preparation of sharing their findings with their selected audience(s).

   "Corporations cannot be trusted to conduct their own oversight of their off-shore drilling operations. Research has shown that, without federal oversight, corporations will not reduce the rate of accidents or prepare well for an eventual spill (Hasson, 2013)."

5. **Synthesizing, Refining, and Redefining.** Reading should be from a variety of sources and texts. This variety often produces conflicting opinions and perspectives. At this point students bring together these perspectives and create new knowledge. This may include the selection of relevant information, the rejection of unnecessary or redundant information, and the evaluation of the validity of what remains and its ability to answer their questions.

   "There are several points of view on who is ultimately responsible for the off-shore drilling disaster. There are arguments for federal jurisdiction, in which the federal government has the final word on whether and to what extent we should have off-shore drilling. There are arguments for state jurisdiction, in which states should be able to make their own decisions about whether and to what extent off-shore drilling should be permitted (National Conference of State Legislatures, 2010). There are also environmental coastal state regulations already in place that affect the extent to which off-shore drilling is permitted (Vann, 2014). Even though there are local entities, like Save Our Shores, that try to lobby against off-shore drilling and also lead clean-up efforts when a spill occurs, their voices are not loud enough to be considered in decision making. Over the years since 2006, off-shore drilling has gained more and more ground through legislation passed at the federal level (Vann, 2014). If that is the case, then the responsibility for the disaster may lie with the federal government."

Inquiry reading engages students at the highest levels of Bloom's Taxonomy. Readers *analyze* by drawing connections among ideas. Readers *evaluate* by posing a solution, taking a stand, or making a decision. Readers *create* by producing new or original work when they formulate solutions and investigate a problem. Inquiry reading focuses on student research of a chosen topic and then reporting out or sharing the results of their inquiry.

TYPES OF INQUIRY READING STRATEGIES

There are a variety of strategies used to conduct inquiry or investigations. For gifted or accelerated readers, and for whom teachers should and must design appropriate reading goals, the following strategies engage these readers, offer them new skills, and challenge their assumptions of what literacy is all about. Gifted readers employ the following set of skills, which are leveraged by several types of inquiry-reading strategies:

1. Gifted readers anticipate meaning based on visual clues.
2. Gifted readers use prior knowledge and experience, personal identification, and reader purpose.
3. Gifted readers are aware of the cognitive processing of text for information or concept gathering. They link the present text with what they have previously read, and as a result, they form or develop concepts (Catron, 1986, p. 136).

Consider the vehicles of enhanced comprehension that lead readers to the solutions and conclusions they seek during inquiry. The following offers teachers and learners a great return on their investment.

Socratic Questioning

Socratic questioning has its roots in pedagogy of Socrates, the 4th-century philosopher whose method of teaching was to ask his students questions in order to help them discover answers. Focused on asking higher-level questions, Socratic questioning adds a deeper level of critical thinking by sifting through all the gathered information, forming a connection to students' prior knowledge, and transforming that new knowledge in a self-directed and complex way. This strategy helps students become more active and engaged learners.

Several formats of Socratic questioning are employed in education settings.

Socratic Seminar or Circle

The Socratic seminar or circle is a whole-class approach to questioning based on a preselected text. The seminar or circle is student-led and creates rich discussion. The teacher takes a backseat to the discussion after carefully

dents to participate in the thoughtful and purposeful examina-
lex topics in respectful discourse. This preparation takes time
the part of the teacher and must be embedded in daily instruc-
... or students to effectively engage in a Socratic seminar or circle.
There are resources to help teachers prepare for a Socratic seminar or circle
at the end of this chapter.

Socratic Critical Questions

Socratic critical questions are different types of questions that, when used in
conjunction, elicit the discovery of knowledge through the probing of the
teacher. Here are the seven types (Intel, 2007) of critical questions with
examples:

1. Clarification questions:

   "Can you give us an example?"
   "Can you describe that in another way?"

2. Questions about an initial question or issue:

   "What is your first reaction to this question?"
   "What can we assume based on this question?"

3. Assumption questions:

   "What are you assuming by saying this?"
   "This is what I think you are saying."

4. Reason and evidence questions:

   "Could you explain your reason for this statement?"
   "Why do you think this is true?"

5. Origin or source questions:

   "Opinions are usually based on something or someone. What is
   yours based on?"
   "What caused you to feel this way?"

6. Implication and consequence questions:

   "If that is true, then how might that affect what happens next?"
   "What is another way this could happen?"

7. Viewpoint questions:

   "What would someone who disagrees with your opinion say instead?"
   "If someone else did not have this experience, then what might
   they think?"

Socratic questioning can be used within the expressed context of a stated inquiry, or it can be used to dive more deeply into informational or literary texts as part of a traditional classroom.

Shared Inquiry

Shared inquiry is a strategy developed by the Great Books Foundation (GBF) as a way for participants to engage in an "active search for the meaning of a work that everyone in the group has read" (GBF, 2014, p. 2). The purpose of shared inquiry is to stimulate a group of readers to read actively, articulate questions effectively, and listen and respond to one another respectfully and with deep understanding. The needs and skills of gifted readers—to anticipate meaning based on visual clues; to use prior knowledge and experience, personal identification, and reader purpose; and to link the present text with what the reader has previously read to form or develop concepts—are fully realized during shared inquiry.

You can use shared inquiry as the primary method for the Junior Great Books or as part of your own exploration of chosen texts. According to the GBF, the following steps are the basic methodology of shared inquiry:

1. Choose an appropriate text to study. Choose a reading that addresses questions that people in all times and places have pondered (e.g., "the nature of the good, the true, and the beautiful; the relationship of the individual to society; the meaning of justice; and the implications of mortality").
2. Read the text carefully before participating in the discussion.
3. Discuss the ideas in the selection and explore them fully.
4. Support interpretations of the text with evidence from the work.
5. Listen carefully to other participants and respond to them directly.
6. Expect the leader (teacher) to mainly ask questions rather than offer his or her own interpretations of the text (GBF, 2014, pp. 8–9).

The role of the teacher is discussion leader and discourse facilitator. Posing an opening question about the reading is the important first step. It should be a question that the teacher herself does not have an answer to. The teacher or discussion leader should model authentic curiosity about the reading and lead students or participants in substantive discourse as they deeply investigate the text. Additional resources about shared inquiry are included at the end of the chapter.

CROSS-CONTENT APPLICATIONS OF INQUIRY READING

The literacy strategy of inquiry reading can and should be applied beyond the English language arts classroom. Inquiry reading is a "nesting strategy" in which the parent strategy (inquiry reading) shelters a variety of already-cited cross-content literacy strategies. For example, the following cross-content strategies are nestled within inquiry reading:

- Reread
- Activate prior knowledge
- Use context clues
- Infer
- Think aloud
- Summarize
- Make predictions
- Visualize
- Evaluate understanding
- Question the text
- Paraphrase
- Annotate the text
- Set a reader purpose
- Make text connections (text to self, text to text, text to the world)

How can we symbolize meaning in content areas besides reading? The primary goal of reading instruction is transference to every content area, context, and opportunity to engage with text. Inquiry reading answers the "why" questions as we investigate the symbolism in great literature, the big questions in science, the moral and pivotal decisions made by leaders in history, the political metaphors in fairy tales and tall tales, and the value of the aesthetic in the arts. Curiosity is fed by inquiry. Teach your students to question the status quo in any content area, and you give them the world.

ELEMENTARY INQUIRY

Developing a culture of inquiry begins early. As early as kindergarten, children can and should be engaged in asking and then answering the bigger questions. As a teacher, are you prepared to guide inquiry with the 6-year-old whose biggest question may be "Why is the sky blue?" Believe it or not, that is a big question and leads naturally into a full-blown inquiry.

Young gifted children naturally ask more questions than most parents and teachers are prepared to answer. Leverage this natural tendency by allowing your first graders to drive the inquiry with their questions. So why is the sky blue anyway?

At the elementary level, teachers set the stage for inquiry by first planning for effective questioning. Even though young gifted students naturally ask questions, they may not be equipped to work through the inquiry process beyond their initial questioning. The process includes the following:

1. Plan the room arrangement and resources needed. Rows of desks are normally not conducive to conversation, let alone investigation. Inquiry is collaborative in nature, and every student should be able to see the others during questioning. Consider the resources your students will need to answer their questions. Provide access to a variety of texts, both on- and offline.

2. Plan for how you will deal with silence or uncertainty. As students begin to engage in questioning and shared inquiry, there may be moments of silence or uncertainty. It's tempting to jump into those silences yourself because it is uncomfortable. Silence and uncertainty are normal parts of the process. Explain this to your students so that they know that the silence will help them work the inquiry.

3. Plan the ground rules. Inquiry at the questioning stage should be free-flowing and uninterrupted whenever possible. Set ground rules, like "No raising your hand before you speak" or "Always respond to a peer before stating your own opinion or asking another question." Students will need to practice these new rules.

4. Plan the initial question. Inquiry begins with a question that doesn't have a straightforward answer. This question can come from the students or from your own questioning of source material. You will not be able to control what comes next after you pose this first question, but then your job as facilitator will be set in motion.

5. Plan how you will refocus student attention and engagement. Inquiry needs to stay focused if it is to be effective. Young gifted readers may ask a lot of questions, but they may not always stay on topic or know how to move their discussion forward. Teachers need to consider how they will intervene and ask either probing or redirection questions in order to steer the discourse through their inquiry.

6. Plan how you will respond to student answers. As young gifted readers learn how to hone their questioning and inquiry skills, inevitably they may give answers that are either less than expected or contrary to your own perspective toward an issue. Plan to withhold judgment in order not to squash their question and answer generation. Instead, ask clarifying questions to encourage them to provide more detail or probing questions that give them a chance to reconsider their initial answers.

Elementary students new to inquiry need models of effective questioning and how to conduct meaningful discourse. Teachers set the foundation of shared inquiry, upon which later grades can build.

SECONDARY INQUIRY

The nature of inquiry reading and learning proposes that students should discover and make meaning for themselves (Witt & Ulmer, 2010). At the middle and high school levels, gifted readers have the opportunity and skill level to engage in robust inquiry. Student-centered and student-led projects across content areas provide middle and high school students opportunities to stretch the questioning muscles they gained during the elementary years.

Secondary students have access to unlimited resources when they begin questioning during their inquiry. Often, they do not know how to manage that information, evaluate its usefulness, and make decisions about their next steps. Teachers can help middle and high school gifted readers get out of the weeds and into the jet stream of inquiry in the following ways:

1. Ask three refocusing questions: *What? So what?* and *Now what?* As students find themselves lost in their inquiry, teachers can interrupt the process in a positive and forward-moving way. Just as parents teach their children to "stop, look, and listen" before crossing the street, teachers can teach their middle and high school students to ask their current question again (What?), then decide if it is still advancing their inquiry (So what?), and finally consider in which direction the inquiry should advance next (Now what?).

2. Create a concept map of the inquiry. Learning how to manage all of the information gathered as a result of inquiry can be daunting to gifted middle and high school students. Teachers can provide an organizational tool or graphic organizer to help them make sense of the mess and display the information in a way that helps them make meaning of it all. A concept map helps show the connections of the information. A table can help keep the sources of their information organized.

3. Write an executive summary. Large-scale inquiries can be especially unwieldy and difficult to analyze, synthesize, and finally evaluate. Teachers can provide students with instruction to write an executive summary of the key points of the inquiry at several times along the way. Wolpert-Gawron (2016) suggests some structure for executive summary writing with middle and high school students.

   • Summarize the main points of the issue.

- Analyze the most important points.
- Recommend a solution.

When writing an executive summary, students should be encouraged to do the following:

- Keep language strong and positive.
- Write no more than two pages.
- Use different text structures: subtitles, bold fonts, bullets, and so on.
- Write in short, readable paragraphs.

In this way students are able to summarize the progress of their inquiry and begin to prepare how they will share their findings with a predetermined audience.

HOW TO EVALUATE INQUIRY READING

As in all assessment, we align our expectations to the desired outcomes. When we evaluate a strategy, we evaluate the students' ability to effectively use that strategy and whether they are able to do that in a self-regulating way. We can align our expectations to product and process assessment, as well as standards assessment.

Product and Process Assessment

The "product" of inquiry reading is the student work produced as a result of this strategy. For example, if the product of Socratic questioning is a Socratic seminar or circle, then we would evaluate students' ability to participate fully and effectively in discussion. A discussion protocol may be devised to monitor students' speaking, reasoning, listening, preparation, or a combination of these for discussion.

If we are assessing and evaluating students' engagement in shared inquiry, then we are looking at the process inherent to this strategy. To what extent do students follow the steps in shared inquiry? Assessing a "process" may include both student self-evaluation and peer evaluation because this does not happen in isolation. As we encourage students to self-regulate, the use of self-evaluation and peer evaluation offers us insight to students' development as inquisitors.

Standards Assessment

Using inquiry reading often helps students to meet multiple standards in the one task of inquiry (Harada & Coatney, 2013). Consider the following content grade-level standards in light of inquiry reading strategies:

• CCSS.ELA-LITERACY.RI.3.6: Distinguish their own point of view from that of the author of a text.
• CCSS.ELA-LITERACY.RH.6–8.8: Distinguish among fact, opinion, and reasoned judgment in a text.
• CCSS.ELA-LITERACY.RST.11–12.9: Synthesize information from a range of sources (e.g., texts, experiments, simulations) into a coherent understanding of a process, phenomenon, or concept, resolving conflicting information when possible. (CCSSO, 2018)

When designing lesson objectives or learning targets, use the inquiry-reading strategy as the condition under which the standard will be met. For example, "Using inquiry reading with a self-selected informational text as part of a student investigation, students will distinguish among fact, opinion, and reasoned judgment in that text." Your assessment will then be designed to evaluate this objective or learning target.

Gifted and accelerated readers are expected to make progress alongside their typically developing peers. They are not exempt from a standards-based education, and it is important to demonstrate how strategies to meet the needs of gifted learners do indeed also meet the content standards.

* * *

From the Expert
Joseph Renzulli, board of trustees distinguished professor, Neag School of Education, University of Connecticut

Within a standards-based system of instruction, can teachers extend those standards for gifted readers (based on content provided by Joseph Renzulli from Renzulli & Waicunas, 2016)?

In the age of standards-based education, gifted readers may not experience the achievement growth anticipated of all students. Traditional approaches and a focus on the basic curriculum do not always produce positive results in both achievement and joyful learning for gifted students. In order to minimize boredom and disengagement to improve both achievement and creative productivity, we recommend applying the Schoolwide Enrichment Model (SEM) to infuse the three Es (enjoyment, engagement, and enthusiasm for learning) into the more traditional culture and climate of a school.

What does it mean to infuse the three Es into an existing curriculum for gifted readers?

Simply stated, it means to:

- review and select highly engaging enrichment-based activities related to particular topics,
- inject them into the curriculum to make the topics more interesting, and
- provide support and encouragement for individuals and small groups who would like to extend their pursuit of the enrichment activities.

We can employ the three types of enrichment activities to advanced reading instruction in order to extend the standards. For example, first identify the relevant standards for your unit of study:

- K.C.1. Understand how individuals are similar and different.
- K.C.1.1. Explain similarities in self and others.
- K.C.1.2. Explain the elements of culture (how people speak, how people dress, foods they eat, etc.).
- Visual Standards: Relate artistic ideas and works with societal, cultural, and historical context to deepen understanding.

Layer the state content-area standards with the NAGC (2010) *Pre-K–Grade 12 Gifted Programming Standards*.

- 3.1.4. Educators design differentiated curricula that incorporate advanced, conceptually challenging, in-depth, distinctive, and complex content for students with gifts and talents.
- 3.5.3. Educators use curriculum for deep explorations of cultures, languages, and social issues related to diversity.

Keeping these standards in mind, teachers plan and prepare a variety of Type I enrichment activities, to which gifted readers will respond: websites and digital sources showing images, customs, and traditional celebrations from different countries, as well as books (literary and informational) for readers to explore. Artifacts from various cultures are selected and made accessible to students. Speakers are invited to provide relevant information and learning experiences. Responses to these texts and materials could be gathered by asking the following questions:

- What did you learn today that was new for you?
- What was the most exciting or interesting?
- Is there anything you still wonder about?

Type II enrichment activities that keep these standards in mind offer students the chance to see and question the differences between themselves and other cultures and allow them to dig more deeply into what they have discovered. The focus here is on thinking and feeling. Teachers can use the enrichment activities to move gifted readers forward and engage with more advanced content in an area of interest. These activities include the development of the following:

- creative thinking and problem solving, critical thinking, and affective processes;
- a wide variety of specific how-to-learn skills;
- skills in the appropriate use of advanced-level reference materials; and
- written, oral, and visual communication skills.

Gifted readers can respond to open-ended questions that will facilitate their responses to text. They can make an analysis by comparing the elements of culture and languages. They can evaluate relevant personal experiences they've had with the culture or language. They can interpret and connect parts of a culture that they believe is most like their own. They can imagine what they think life might be like if they had grown up in one of the other countries or cultures.

Type I and Type II activities help illustrate to what extent standards have been met. Type III enrichment activities then help students to finish independent projects and complete any unmet standards. During these activities, students take more control of their own learning. They are the directors, the problem solvers, the investigators. They have been prepared at this point with any prerequisite skills necessary for independent investigation.

Depending on their areas of interest within the unit, students may create a presentation and become the teacher; design a brochure or website; take a poll of favorite food or place; create an advertisement or television show; or create an artistic expression, a digital story from a culture or country, or a gallery walk to showcase representative aspects of a culture or country. The goal during Type III is to create something to share with a real-world audience.

Infusion of enrichment activities may not be possible for every topic, course, or standard, but whenever possible it makes learning more engaging and creates an enthusiasm for learning that may not be gained from more traditional learning experiences. The basic guidelines for successful infusion in order to bolster the content-level standards for gifted readers are the following:

- Select an activity that does not always have a single, predetermined correct answer.

- Find things that students do rather than sit and listen to.
- Give students choices that they will enjoy pursuing.
- Select activities that have various levels of challenge that interested readers can escalate.

* * *

ASSIGNMENT(S)

1. Review the *Shared Inquiry Handbook* provided by the Great Books Foundation (2014).
2. Watch the Junior Great Books (2011) *Shared Inquiry Discussion* Vimeo video.
3. Review the sample shared-inquiry lesson plan "Leave It to Beavers?" from the Great Books Foundation (2017).
4. Consider a story you are teaching in your class right now. Using the shared-inquiry strategy, design a lesson (whatever format you prefer) following the instructional routines demonstrated in the shared-inquiry strategy.

REFLECT

How can you use inquiry reading to raise expectations for gifted and accelerated students in order to show growth throughout the year?

REFERENCES

Catron, R. M. (1986). Developing the potential of the gifted reader. *Theory Into Practice*, 25, 134–140.

Council of Chief State School Officers (CCSSO). (2018). English language arts standards. *Common Core State Standards Initiative*. Retrieved April 22, 2018, from http://www.corestandards.org/ELA-Literacy/

Great Books Foundation (GBF). (2014). *Shared inquiry handbook*. Chicago: Great Books Foundation. Retrieved March 1, 2018, from https://www.greatbooks.org/wp-content/uploads/2014/12/Shared-Inquiry-Handbook.pdf

Great Books Foundation. (2017). *Shared inquiry lesson plan for "Leave it to beavers?"* Retrieved from https://www.greatbooks.org/wp-content/uploads/2016/07/Leave-It-to-Beavers-Lesson-Plan.pdf

Harada, V. H., & Coatney, S. (Eds.). (2013). *Inquiry and the common core: Librarians and teachers designing teaching for learning*. Santa Barbara, CA: ABC-CLIO Solutions.

Hasson, N. (2013). Deep water offshore oil exploration regulation: The need for a global environmental regulation regime, 4 Wash. & Lee J. Energy, *Climate & Env't.*, 277.

Intel. (2007). Designing effective projects: Questioning: The Socratic questioning technique. *Intel Teach Program*. Retrieved March 28, 2018, from https://www.intel.com/content/dam/

www/program/education/us/en/documents/project-design/strategies/dep-question-socratic.
   pdf
Junior Great Books. (2011). Shared inquiry discussion. *Vimeo*. Retrieved from https://vimeo.
   com/16260234
National Association for Gifted Children (NAGC). (2010, November). *NAGC Pre-K–Grade 12
   Gifted Programming Standards: A Blueprint for Quality Gifted Education Programs*. Washington, DC: Author. Retrieved from http://www.nagc.org/sites/default/files/standards/K-
   12%20standards%20booklet.pdf
National Conference of State Legislatures, (2010). 2010 Offshore drilling legislation. Retrieved
   from http://www.ncsl.org/research/energy/2010-oil-drilling-legislation.aspx
Renzulli, J. A., & Waicunas, N. (2016). An infusion-based approach to enriching the standards-
   driven curriculum. In S. M. Reis (Ed.), *Reflections on gifted education* (pp. 411–428).
   Waco, TX: Prufrock Press.
Vann, A. (2014). Offshore oil and gas development: Legal framework. RL33404. Congression-
   al Research Service, Washington, DC. https://www.fas.org/sgp/crs/misc/R40806.pdf.
Witt, C., & Ulmer, J. (2010). The impact of inquiry-based learning on the academic achieve-
   ment of middle school students. *Western AAAE Research Conference Proceedings*, 269.
   Retrieved from http://www.academia. edu/724764
Wolpert-Gawron, H. (2016). *DIY project based learning for math and science*. New York:
   Routledge.
Wood, P. (2008). Reading instruction with gifted and talented readers. *Gifted Child Today*,
   31(3), 16–25.

Chapter Eight

Flexible Grouping

"Grouping is a vehicle educators can use to allow gifted children access to learning at the level and complexity they need."—National Association for Gifted Children (NAGC, 2009)

SCENARIO

Twenty-four second graders huddle together for morning meeting on the brightly colored carpet that revealed the planets in the solar system. Ms. Cesta loves these moments at the beginning of the school day to come together as a community and review some of the skills they have learned throughout the year. It is a way to start the day with respect for one another and honor each other's gifts. After their daily greeting and community-building activity, Ms. Cesta introduces the skill review for the day: "Good morning class! Today is Tuesday, March 10. Do you remember how to sound out a CVC word? We will see how many we can read in the *Mig the Pig* big book today!"

After reading *Mig the Pig* together on the carpet, Ms. Cesta transitions into guided reading. With 24 students, classroom management is key to making guided reading groups work. There are four groups of six students, in which Ms. Cesta has carefully placed one of her four advanced readers. This way, the advanced readers can be helpers to those who may struggle with the center activity. It's a logistics matter. After all, 24 second graders aren't always easy to manage. Ms. Cesta believes that all students benefit from heterogeneous groupings and that her advanced readers are like leavening in bread: They help everyone rise.

Nick is reading on a second-grade level N; Jacob is reading on a third-grade level Q; Amanda is reading on a third-grade level N; Abbie is reading

d-grade level M. They are grouped with students who are either
grade level or below grade level. What started as a way to help
___ manage her guided reading groups and centers later becomes a
hindrance. Nick and Jacob disrupt their groups and refuse to follow the
guidelines of their centers. Amanda and Abbie withdraw and retreat into
books they bring from home. They are bored. They learned CVC words and
Mig the Pig when they were 3. Now what?

One of the key components of an advanced reading program for gifted readers is flexible grouping. Whether gifted readers are served in a traditional or
inclusive classroom or in a gifted resource classroom, magnet program, or
separate school, their needs as readers who require advanced instruction are
better met when they are grouped in a purposeful way. There are several
ways teachers can group gifted readers to accomplish the intended goals:
ability grouping, interest grouping, and cluster grouping.

Although ability grouping is a traditional approach to grouping students
and remains a controversial issue in education, gifted readers benefit from
homogeneous grouping practices. In order to facilitate the advanced reading
program goals of creative reading, critical reading, and inquiry reading,
grouping gifted readers together allows for appropriate curriculum and instruction for those who learn at a faster rate than their typical peers (Wood,
2008).

Grouping provides teachers with the setting in which differentiation can
be effective. Grouping should always be done to enable readers to move
forward in their learning. Whether the purpose is skill based, interest related,
an author study, or a literature circle, gifted readers prefer and should be
grouped with peers who work at the same level and with the same task
persistence. Teachers can use grouping as a way to allow gifted readers
equitable access to learning at their level with the depth and complexity they
need (Tiesco, 2003).

Teachers use flexible grouping as a within-class accommodation for
gifted students. It is a way to differentiate the learning environment so that
they can work with others like them. Consider the different groupings that
support the advanced reading instruction goals appropriate for gifted and
accelerated readers.

NAGC PRE-K–GRADE 12 GIFTED PROGRAMMING STANDARDS

Flexible grouping is not proposed for the sake of grouping. It is what happens
in the groupings that matters. Flexible grouping of gifted readers aligns with
the following standards:

1.3.1. Educators provide a variety of research-based grouping practices for students with gifts and talents that allow them to interact with individuals of various gifts, talents, abilities, and strengths.

4.2.2. Educators provide opportunities for interaction with intellectual and artistic/creative peers as well as with chronological-age peers.

ABILITY GROUPS

Grouping is only as good as what is done in the group. The decision to group students according to ability is intentional and purposeful. This is not "tracking" or permanent homogeneous groups. Gifted and accelerated readers benefit from ability grouping for particular tasks. One way that ability grouping can be used to advance a gifted reader's learning is to use it alongside compacting the curriculum. Teachers can use this approach to summarize and condense the curriculum, so that the gifted readers can move on to more advanced reading instruction (Sisk, 2009).

Grouping by ability begins with identifying your high readers. If you are grouping within a traditional inclusive classroom, then you may only have one group of high-ability readers. If you are grouping within a gifted or accelerated classroom, then you can also differentiate by ability because that class will also be reading on a variety of levels. The purpose behind grouping readers by ability should be to facilitate appropriate differentiation. During guided reading, both curriculum and instruction for gifted readers can be differentiated. The goal is to provide gifted readers access to advanced content and skills. What happens in this group should be different from what happens in other groups.

At the secondary level, ability groups can be formed permanently by course level. For example, gifted readers may be placed in advanced sections of ELA courses or Advanced Placement (AP) courses. The attributes of these types of courses naturally lend themselves to ability grouping for advanced instruction. However, even within these contexts, there may be a variety of reading levels. In order to meet the needs of gifted readers at the secondary level through ability grouping, teachers should engage in curriculum compacting to address their advanced needs.

What Does This Look Like During Reading Instruction?

After screening to determine who your highest readers are, administer a pretest on the upcoming content to determine if and to what extent these readers have already mastered the knowledge and skills. The results of the pretest lead to curriculum compacting.

There are three steps to curriculum compacting: pretesting, eliminate content or skills the students have already mastered, and replace the eliminated content or skills with alternative topics or skills. Gifted readers will then work with the teacher to select alternative activities. They may work on an independent reading project of their own design, practice advanced reading skills with advanced texts, or engage in an enrichment activity that the rest of the class is not yet ready to pursue (Smutny, Walker, & Meckstroth, 1997). Ability groups offer an opportunity for in-class or in-grade acceleration for gifted readers.

INTEREST GROUPS

In addition to ability grouping, another way to group gifted students is by interests. Interest groups can be formed within a traditional classroom or used to group students together in a gifted classroom. Interest groups are a way to differentiate content more effectively and adapt curriculum to the needs of gifted readers. Interest groups can also be formed across grade levels or used in multi-age classroom settings. For those readers recognized as underachieving gifted students, membership in interest groups removes any stigma of underachievement, even among other gifted readers. The opportunity to connect their learning experiences with peers of like interests is an effective motivator.

For students who experience a sense of isolation due to their intense interest in a particular topic or subject matter that their peers may not understand or share (Trezise, 1978), gifted readers can fit in with those who share their same love for all things Tolkien or the mummification techniques of the early Egyptians. Interest groups span the ability spectrum and offer a shared learning experience to a diverse group of readers. Gifted students often complain that they are not able to pursue topics of interest in favor of the mind-numbing exercise of engaging in skills they have already mastered. Using interest groups as a flexible grouping strategy combats both boredom and underachievement.

What Does This Look Like During Reading Instruction?

In the earlier grades, interest groups can function more like interest centers. Consider designing interest centers during the reading block that allow readers to explore topics of interest to them while still connecting to literacy. First, it is important to gauge students' interests before designing an interest group or center. Prominent gifted educators and researchers Sally Reis and Joseph Renzulli developed two interest assessments that give teachers valuable insight into the interests of their students.

The "If I Ran the School Interest Inventory" (Reis & Siegle, 2002) helps students and teachers find areas of interest in which students who may be underachieving can work on together. This brief interest inventory provides an interest snapshot. The "Interest-a-Lyzer" (Renzulli, 1997) has two formats: one for earlier grades and one for middle grades. The "Interest-a-Lyzer" takes a little longer to complete, but it is well worth it. It offers teachers targeted insight into the interests of their gifted readers and helps students examine and focus their interests. The results from either or both of these interest inventories provide students with creative and productive outlets for expressing their interests. Teachers can then design interest groups or centers that stimulate their interests.

Include the application of advanced reading skills and texts when using interest groups or centers. Make sure that, even if the readers are grouped by interest, they still have access to advanced content and materials so that this type of grouping moves them forward. For example, if a group of sixth-grade gifted readers all like or want to read the same book, then they can work together in a book circle or design nontraditional ways to explore the social or political themes in the book; a moral dilemma presented by the author; or advanced skills, like voice, character motivation, and identifying the plot points of the hero's journey.

CLUSTER GROUPS

Cluster groups are a type of flexible grouping in which at least five gifted readers in a grade level are grouped together in one classroom with a heterogeneous set of peers. Enrichment clusters allow gifted readers to become involved in learning that is inductive, self-selected, and investigative. In an enrichment cluster, the teacher's role is a facilitator, turning the responsibility for creative and investigative activity over to the students (Renzulli, Gentry, & Reis, 2007). The rationale behind the use of cluster groups relies on the fact that gifted students benefit from and often prefer to work with intellectual peers who display similar learning characteristics (Rogers, 1998). Gifted readers placed together in cluster groups focus on developing advanced reading and writing skills.

What Does This Look Like During Reading Instruction?

Two ways in which cluster groups can be employed during reading instruction include skill groups and reading and writing workshops. Skill groups are short-term placements in which gifted readers can be taught together more advanced reading skills or they can be used for grade-level acceleration in reading. This skill group works toward mastery, and once they achieve mastery, they move onto another skill level.

Reading and writing workshops offer gifted readers an opportunity to read, write, edit, and comment on each other's work much like an adult authors' critique group. Time should be set aside to read, write, share, de-

conference with both the teacher and peers. Readers can keep
ıd writing logs, create their own reading and writing goals, and
ue as a reflective exercise.

TEACHER'S ROLE WITH FLEXIBLE GROUPING

Teachers who opt to use flexible grouping practices for gifted readers should
be trained or prepared to make these types of adaptations to their curriculum
and instructional routines. The most obvious yet effective shift for the teacher is to move from being a "director" of learning to a "facilitator" of learning.
In addition, it is recommended that teachers of gifted readers know how to:

- recognize and nurture gifted behaviors and characteristics with reading,
- understand the social-emotional needs of gifted readers,
- allow students to demonstrate previous mastery of concepts and compact
  the curriculum accordingly,
- provide opportunities for flexible pacing of new material,
- incorporate readers' interests into their independent studies,
- facilitate exploration and research investigations, and
- provide a variety of flexible grouping options for the whole class (Winebrenner & Devlin, 1992).

CONCLUSION

Research suggests that gifted readers are more likely to choose more challenging tasks when they can work with other gifted readers (Kulik & Kulik,
1990). The myths that grouping gifted students is damaging to the self-
esteem of struggling readers or that it creates an elite group of readers have
no foundation in research. If the purpose is to differentiate instruction in such
a way that students can reach their potential and show growth, then flexible
grouping is effective during reading instruction. It is one way to reach our
established reading program goals discussed in this book.

* * *

From the Expert
Dr. Jane Gangi, professor of education, Mount Saint Mary College

Those of us in literacy and language arts focus on transmediation, which
means recasting text from one symbol system to another. For example, after
reading a narrative, readers could, in response, create a travel brochure, reader's theater, book jacket, or Animoto or YouTube video. They can write

letters to the author, the illustrator (mail them or not), or one of the characters. They could create a map, such as of Narnia from *The Chronicles of Narnia*, or write a diary entry from one character's point of view.

For nonfiction, students can create a website on a topic or a poster or a timeline or a graph. They can write advocacy and activist letters. They can write the résumé, obituary, or news article of a historical figure. For poetry, they can create a choral reading, picturing writing (a watercolor and crayon resist technique), or image making (a collage technique) in response to all kinds of themes and topics. Other artforms for response include storytelling, dance, sculpture, film, and music.

Teachers can incorporate creative reading experiences with their whole class and at the same time meet the needs of gifted or keenly interested readers. Offering multimodal pathways allows accelerated readers to self-differentiate. For example, I shared songbooks with first graders. One song in particular has been especially effective: "Siempre Abuelita" by Trish Hinojosa. The song is sung in both English and Spanish and is about a child's special relationship with her grandmother. One first grader began composing and singing her own songs. At the end of the session, when we asked first graders what they had learned about themselves, she exclaimed, "I learned I am a songwriter!"

It's also important to have texts that might be considered at a higher grade level. A former student remembers reading *Oliver Twist* in sixth grade. My own study of what writers read in childhood showed that Maya Angelou read Shakespeare in elementary school and Debra Dickerson, the daughter of a former sharecropper and writer for *The Nation* and *Mother Jones*, read Maya Angelou's *I Know Why the Caged Bird Sings* in elementary school—five times. She said, "It had never occurred to me that blacks could write books. With this discovery, my desire for serious modern literature burst into flame. I lost myself in the Harlem Renaissance." Beverly Cleary listened to her mother read *A Christmas Carol* before she was 5. Just the words "'Scrooge and Marley,'" Cleary writes, were "mysterious and filled with foreboding." Zora Neale Hurston read and loved *Gulliver's Travels* in elementary school.

Do elementary school readers understand the "mature" elements of *I Know Why the Caged Bird Sings*? Probably not. But books like those can and often are revisited, the reader creating deeper levels of meaning with each reading.

* * *

ASSIGNMENT

Conduct an interest inventory with your students so that you can make informed choices about grouping. Access the "If I Ran the School Interest Inventory" (Reis & Siegle, 2002) and the "Interest-a-Lyzer" (Renzulli, 1997), and then create a class profile of your students' interests. Using the interest profile, organize your readers into interest groups. You can access both of these inventories here:

- "If I Ran the School Interest Inventory," http://www.prufrock.com/Assets/ ClientPages/pdfs/SEM_Web_Resources/ If%20I%20Ran%20the%20School%20Interest%20Survey.pdf
- "Interest-a-Lyzer," http://www.prufrock.com/assets/clientpages/pdfs/sem _web_resources/interest-a-lyzer.pdf

REFLECT

Consider how you currently group students during reading instruction. Define the purpose behind your grouping strategy. Then reflect on whether those purposes meet the needs of your gifted readers.

REFERENCES

Kulik, J. A., & Kulik, C.-L. C. (1990). Ability grouping and gifted students. In N. Colangelo & G. Davis (Eds.), *Handbook of gifted education* (pp. 178–196). Boston: Allyn & Bacon.

National Association of Gifted Children (NAGC). (2009, March). *Position statement: Grouping.* Washington, DC: Author. Retrieved from https://www.nagc.org/sites/default/files/ Position%20Statement/Grouping%20Position%20Statement.pdf

Reis, S. M., & Siegle, D. (2002). If I ran the school: An interest inventory. Retrieved from https://nrcgt.uconn.edu/wp-content/uploads/sites/953/2015/07/cc_ranschool.pdf

Renzulli, J. (1997). *Interest-a-lyzer family of instruments: A manual for teachers.* Waco, TX: Prufrock Press.

Renzulli, J. S., Gentry, M., & Reis, S. (2007). Enrichment cluster for developing creativity and high-end learning. *Gifted and Talented International, 22,* 39–46.

Rogers, K. (1998). Using current research to make "good" decisions about grouping. *NASSP Bulletin, 82,* 38–46.

Sisk, D. (2009). Myth 13: The regular classroom teacher can "go it alone." *Gifted Child Quarterly, 53*(4), 269–271.

Smutny, J. F., Walker, S. Y., & Meckstroth, E. A. (1997). *Teaching young gifted children in the regular classroom: Identifying, nurturing, and challenging ages 4–9.* Minneapolis: Free Spirit.

Tiesco, C. (2003). Ability grouping is not just tracking anymore. *Roeper Review, 26,* 29–36.

Trezise, R. L. (1978). What about a reading programme for the gifted? *Reading Teacher, 31,* 742–747.

Winebrenner, S., & Devlin, B. (1992, Fall). Cluster grouping fact sheet: How to provide full-time services for gifted students on existing budgets. *National Research Center on the Gifted and Talented Newsletter, University of Connecticut.*

Wood, P. F. (2008). Reading instruction with gifted and talented readers: A series of unfortunate events or a sequence of auspicious results? *Gifted Child Today, 31*(3), 16–24.

A Final Word About Differentiation and Gifted Readers

At this point the rationale for designing literacy instruction around the needs of gifted readers is well established. Admittedly, differentiation takes more time and effort than following the basic curriculum, and for some teachers that may be a stumbling block. The central assumption of this book is that, if you're reading it, then you are already at least interested in doing something different to meet the needs of your students.

Although differentiation is more common now than in past decades, teachers are not always well prepared to differentiate effectively. Knowledge about differentiation alone does not translate into action. The skill of differentiation must be practiced and supported. Hopefully you have gained both knowledge and skill with this book to meet the needs of the gifted and accelerated readers in your charge.

About the Author

Vicki Caruana, PhD, is an associate professor of education at Mount Saint Mary College in Newburgh, New York, where she also serves as the gifted program coordinator. Vicki's teaching career began in a middle school learning disabilities resource room, where she taught literacy. By her third year of teaching, she discovered that there was a group of 10 students in her resource room whose abilities were considerably higher than any of her other students with learning disabilities. No one knew what to do with them. The goal, just as for any student with a learning disability, was to close the gap between achievement and ability and provide opportunities to help them develop coping skills that transfer to other content areas and contexts. Puzzled about how to help these students, Vicki decided to go back to school and obtain her certification in gifted education to learn more about this population and what they needed in order to succeed.

After completing only three courses required for certification, Vicki realized it was not enough to know how to change her teaching practices effectively in a way that met the needs of gifted students, especially those with learning disabilities. She enrolled in a master's program in gifted education and focused her research on gifted students with learning disabilities—those we now call "twice exceptional," or 2E. At that time Vicki began to teach gifted enrichment classes at the middle school, again in the area of literacy. She created a curriculum that focused on a combination of enrichment and acceleration around the goals of creative, critical, and inquiry reading.

Vicki's love for curriculum development became the focus of her work with students whose needs are not typical. When she embarked on her doctorate, she chose curriculum and instruction as her degree program. Well versed in individualized planning, specially designed instruction, and standards-based education, Vicki effectively plans meaningful learning experiences for students with varying abilities and teaches others how to do the same.

When Vicki served as the coordinator of a center for gifted studies in a middle school in a large district in Florida, she was able to apply her curriculum-design expertise to help create an integrated curriculum experience in the center. Later, and now as the founding coordinator of the gifted graduate program at her college, Vicki works closely with surrounding districts to prepare teachers for effective differentiation practices that foster achievement gains for gifted readers. To learn more, visit Vicki's website and blog at https://vickicaruana.net.